THE SOUL ADVENTURE GUIDE

---

7 Principles for Successful Living

FEATURING MY TRUE **HOLLYWOOD** STORY

Bobby Fite

SOUL INNOVATIONS
DALLAS, TEXAS

SOUL INNOVATIONS
DALLAS, TEXAS

Some of the names in this book have been changed to protect the privacy of the individuals involved.

Photo on page 8 licensed by:
Warner Bros. Entertainment Inc. All Rights Reserved.

ISBN: 978-0-6159788-2-6

Copyright © 2014 by Bobby Fite

All rights reserved. No part of this publication may be reproduced, distributed, or transmitted in any form or by any means, including photocopying, recording, or other electronic or mechanical methods, without the prior written permission of the publisher, except in the case of brief quotations embodied in critical reviews and certain other non-commercial uses permitted by copyright law.

Editor: Jennifer Read Hawthorne
Interior and cover design: Gary A. Rosenberg
   www.thebookcouple.com

Printed in the United States of America

CONTENTS

	Introduction	1
PART ONE	**My True Hollywood Story**	
CHAPTER 1	Lights, Camera, Action	9
CHAPTER 2	Shift Happens	23
PART TWO	**7 Principles for Successful Living**	
CHAPTER 3	Manage Your Estate of Mind	39
CHAPTER 4	Be the Real You	47
CHAPTER 5	See the Big Picture	61
CHAPTER 6	Awaken Your Spiritual Energies	67
CHAPTER 7	Pay Attention to Signs	77
CHAPTER 8	Do the Greater Good for All Concerned	87
CHAPTER 9	Handle Life's Details	93
APPENDIX A	Helping Others—Acts of Kindness	99
APPENDIX B	The Guide to Successful Living	101
APPENDIX C	The Toolbox: Tools, Techniques, and Strategies	103
	Acknowledgments	111

INTRODUCTION

I was eager to get life started. So at the age of nine, I talked my way into the television and film business. It turned out to be a pretty solid move—by age fourteen, I had reached the height of prime-time television as a recurring character on a hit sitcom called *Silver Spoons*.

I next landed a role in a highly anticipated movie from Paramount Pictures called *Explorers*. Directed by one of Hollywood's hottest directors, the film was projected to be a huge blockbuster. Expectations for my future were so bright that my agent and manager were marketing me as the next Tom Cruise.

So it may be hard to believe that, a few years later, I was suffering from devastating depression and contemplating suicide. But that's what happened. You hear people say they can't see the light at the end of the tunnel; I couldn't even see the tunnel.

While this first stage of my life was extremely difficult at times, it led me to the most profound experience of my life and propelled me into a personal spiritual journey that's exceeded all my expectations. This extraordinary "happening" opened my eyes to a far greater reality and led me to learn several key principles—"truths about living," as I like to call them—that forever changed my perspective on this world.

Applying these truths in my own life allowed me to rise from the depths of depression, transcend the boulevard of broken dreams, and achieve a much better life. Today I enjoy a far greater level of peace than ever before. I am happily married to a loving, kind, and supportive wife, and I have developed deeply satisfying friendships.

Spiritually, I have developed an attunement with God that's difficult to express in words, and I've experienced many moments of divine inspiration on my personal spiritual journey.

Professionally, I have distinguished myself as one of the top-producing sales professionals in the U.S. home building industry, having worked for the nation's leading home builders for eleven years and having successfully managed multi-million dollar development projects.

Financially, these principles have led me to create significant prosperity. I now enjoy a very comfortable lifestyle that enables me to live in my dream home and travel to beautiful places.

And if you're willing to apply these same principles in your own life—you *will* create a better life!

Why I Wrote this Book

So why did I leave a successful job to write this book? Was I trying to recapture the glory days of my acting career? Hardly . . . I actually place great value on my privacy and rarely talk about the past. My reason for writing this book is simple: at the lowest point in my life, I made a promise to God. I told him that if he would help me regain my inner strength, I would help someone else do the same in the future.

Over the years, I've privately shared these truths with many individuals that God placed in my path. Then, during a moment of profound spiritual leading, he informed me that it was time

INTRODUCTION

to share my story publicly, with the important lessons I had learned along the way.

The Soul Adventure Guide is my fulfillment of that promise.

What You'll Find in This Book

The Soul Adventure Guide is a unique book—a powerful guide to self-help, life improvement, and personal spiritual growth—that evolved from a compelling true Hollywood story. The strength of this book is that it's grounded in real-life experience, not a bunch of lofty intellectual theories. It's a collection of essential life lessons, practical self-help techniques, key spiritual teachings, and universal principles that are the cornerstones of successful living.

In the past twenty years, I've done my best to live in harmony with these teachings, and as a result, I have experienced significant personal and spiritual growth. I've explored many paths in an effort to find peace, satisfy my adventurous spirit, and create the life of my dreams. This book contains the most essential principles that I've discovered.

Part One is "My True Hollywood Story." In chapter 1, I share my story as it relates to key features of this life-improvement guide. While I realize many readers won't recognize my name, it's my hope that they never forget the message revealed in this story—"Lights, Camera, Action!"

Chapter 2, "Shift Happens," reveals Act Two of my story, when I learned about the lure of materialism—which taught me some of the toughest and most crucial life lessons I've ever had to face. I had to undergo key mental shifts in order to develop a balanced perspective on money, realize economic prosperity, and understand the true meaning of success—all of which I'll share with you in this chapter.

Part Two contains the seven principles or "truths about living" that have transformed my life. We begin exploring those truths in chapter 3, "Manage Your Estate of Mind," in which we will look at the mind as our most important piece of "real estate" and discuss why managing the content of our mind is so vital. We'll also look at practical techniques to simplify this task.

In chapter 4, "Be the Real You," we discover the reasons that millions of people in the world are in a state of inner dis-ease, feeling separated from their true self. I share helpful insights, real-life examples, and practical strategies for increasing personal peace and creating positive self-change. This knowledge will help you create a stronger, more positive personality that's better aligned with who you really are.

In chapter 5, "See the Big Picture," I'll share my perspective on how we can view our earthly lives as the very early stages of an endless adventure. I will present what I believe are the goals for human beings in this life and offer clarity on the process of personal spiritual growth.

Chapter 6 is "Awaken Your Spiritual Energies," in which I reveal our most satisfying human experience and investigate the dramatic trend in America toward personal aspects of spirituality. We will explore the essence of spirituality, the gift of spiritual freedom, and the unique attributes we've been given as independent spiritual beings.

Chapter 7, "Pay Attention to Signs," is where I reveal my most profound life experience, the "happening" that forever changed my perception of this world. Likewise, I offer readers helpful hints on embarking upon or increasing the excitement of their own personal journey.

Chapter 8 is where I discuss one of the most powerful secrets of all time: "Do the Greater Good for All Concerned."

INTRODUCTION

This principle is the key to our spiritual progress and achieving the goals of this lifetime. Once you understand it, making decisions—no matter how challenging—becomes far easier.

Finally, in chapter 9, "Handle Life's Details," I'll talk about the key reasons why we must take care of the details in our lives, and I'll show how doing so impacts our spiritual growth, our relationships, and our overall quality of life. Likewise, we'll discuss the important role of personal organization in simplifying our lives.

All the main points of the book are blended into a simple, easy-to-use section at the end called "The Guide to Successful Living."

❖ ❖ ❖

Successful living demands a holistic approach. We must speak to the deepest needs of our soul, the inner aspects of our mind and self, and the realities of dealing with our fast-paced, materialistic world.

Although certain aspects of my journey are individual, the insights gained, lessons learned, and principles applied are *universal*. If you apply these teachings, you *will* create a deeper, happier, and more satisfying life. Here's what I hope you'll take away from this book:

- Inspiration from my story and the confidence that you too can create a better life

- Clearly defined goals for your life and a simple guide to achieving them

- A sense of excitement, purpose, and direction

- An increased feeling of spiritual freedom

- A deep sense of peace, happiness, and satisfaction with life as you increasingly feel the presence of the spiritual energies within you and begin to embark on or increase the potency of your personal spiritual journey

- Greater prosperity and quality of life achieved by applying these principles in your professional life and avoiding painful lessons regarding money and materialism

I am human and imperfect—still a work in progress. Deeply moved by my having been "selected" for this project, I have stepped way outside my comfort zone to answer this calling. In his book *Inspiration: Your Ultimate Calling*, Wayne Dyer says, "Inspiration is a calling to proceed even though we're unsure of goals or achievements—it may even insist that we go in the direction of uncharted territory." (p. 6)

Our life's journey is like embarking on a whitewater adventure: we greatly benefit from having an experienced guide—one who knows the river and helps us stay balanced in rough waters. Likewise, a skillful guide understands the importance of being in harmony with the flow of the river. Just like a mountain stream, the river of life has a current that's controlled by unseen forces.

If you choose me as your guide, I promise to help you skillfully navigate the waters of adversity and lead you to a better life. I also promise to make the voyage entertaining, tell you a great story, and present life as the exciting personal adventure it should be.

Now, let's get to it.

PART ONE

MY TRUE HOLLYWOOD STORY

Playing James Garner's son (left) in the 1982 movie
The Long Summer of George Adams, Warner Bros. Television.

1
LIGHTS, CAMERA, ACTION!

By age fifteen, I was living a life many people dream about. I had a fast-talking agent in Beverly Hills, a respected L.A. business manager, and a recurring role on a hit sitcom called *Silver Spoons*. Plus, I was performing in movies with some of Hollywood's biggest stars.

Many people have assumed I was a spoiled rich kid from California whose parents got him into the business to show off their prized progeny—a perception that always makes me laugh, because it couldn't be further from the truth. In reality, my true Hollywood story illustrates the power of faith and desire to transform our lives.

Here's what happened to me.

My Story Begins

I was just a red-blooded American kid with a curious mind, an adventurous spirit, and the hope that my life would be exciting. Although I was not born into a world of wealth and privilege, I possessed two things that were far more valuable: the desire to *try* and a willingness to *take some chances* in hopes that something good would happen.

Raised in a town as glamorous as its name—Farmers Branch, Texas—I was the adopted son and only child of a strong-willed working-class family. We lived in a small frame house built in the fifties, where it was common knowledge that the world didn't owe you anything. If you wanted something, you had to go out and earn it.

My dad was an old-school tough guy, born on the kitchen table of a small country house in Saltillo, Texas. Think Clint Eastwood in *Million Dollar Baby*. Feisty out of the womb, he got kicked out of high school for fighting and went to work in the oil fields with his father. As an adult, he coached amateur boxing for twenty-five years and drove a wrecker, repossessing cars to earn a living.

When I was four years old, he tossed me into the boxing ring with a determined competitor in front of a crowd of three hundred spectators. He figured it would help make a man out of me—and in some ways it did.

My mom was the youngest of eight sisters and grew up during the Great Depression. She dreamed of becoming a prosecuting attorney but was forced to drop out of high school to help support the family and care for her sick mother. Eventually, she secured a job at a large bookstore in downtown Dallas, where she worked her way into management and stayed for thirty years. She was a tough lady, which she proved by becoming the first female professional boxing manager in Texas.

One day, as I was expressing a moment of self-doubt, she sat me down, looked me in the eye, and said, "Son, if you don't believe in yourself, why should anyone else believe in you?" It was the last thing I wanted to hear at the moment, but no matter how hard I tried, I couldn't think of a way around it.

This statement really stuck in my head and forced me to become accountable for the results I would produce in life. I realized that it was my responsibility to develop faith in my abilities; no one else could do it for me.

On Sundays, I was given the choice to go to church with family friends or play football. As a highly competitive young man with decent speed, good hands, and a few moves, most days I chose football. One such Sunday, my friends and I were sitting around talking after the game, when one of them said he knew a kid who modeled for the Sears catalog. The kicker was that they paid him thirty-five bucks an hour!

My nine-year-old entrepreneurial spirit immediately kicked in. Now I didn't know this kid, but he didn't sound like anything special. So I asked myself, *Why not me?* I mean seriously, how hard could it be? And it just so happened that I had my eye on a skateboard that cost exactly thirty-five bucks.

So the next day after school, I rushed home and called the largest talent agency in Dallas, the Kim Dawson Agency. I told the sophisticated lady on the phone that I wanted to be a model and was ready to get signed up. She politely informed me that the agency held interviews for *potential* new clients on Thursdays and that I needed to bring a picture.

My next move was the tough part: convincing my mom to take a day off work and drive me to the agency. You see, in my working-class household, you went to work or school unless you were dying. She wanted no part of it. But after three weeks of relentless hounding, she agreed, just to shut me up (I could be very persistent).

When the big day came, I grabbed my humble soccer picture and headed downtown. We arrived to find a waiting room packed full of kids, with mothers straightening their hair and giving last-minute instructions. My mom just wanted to get out of there. After an hour of this drama, my name was finally called—it was time to get down to business.

The receptionist walked me back to meet with an attractive blonde, most likely an ex-model. She asked me questions for about twenty minutes and seemed impressed by my sincerity and determination. I had to be the only kid there who had booked his own meeting.

Then she smiled and said she liked my personality and thought I had an all-American look. She congratulated me on making the cut and handed me the number of a real photographer so I could get some professional pictures taken. When she walked me out to tell my mother, Mom was stunned, looking as if perhaps there had been a mistake. I just looked at her confidently, like, "Yeah I told you so."

The agency didn't send me out much the first year. I got lost in the shuffle with the seventy other kids who actually had experience. Then one day after school, they called to see if I was interested in taking some acting classes. The classes would teach kids how to get cast in TV commercials and acting jobs. It sounded interesting, so I decided to make the pitch when Mom got home from work.

When I told her the classes were 180 bucks, she almost passed out. However, I calmly explained to her, "You have to spend money to make money."

Once I started taking classes, a lady at the agency saw me on tape and thought I might have some talent, so she started sending me out on commercial auditions. Within a few months, I booked my first commercial and worked with a kid who had just appeared in the movie *Jaws*, directed by Steven Spielberg. He was a big deal at the agency and filled me in on the business. That's when I found out they were paying us $1,000 for one day's work!

My auditioning skills got better; I started getting jobs left and right. I soon landed my first acting role, playing James Garner's son in a television movie called *The Long Summer of George Adams*. Then I scored a part in a major film, *The Best Little Whorehouse in Texas*, which starred Burt Reynolds and Dolly Parton. By that point, I had become the most successful child actor in Texas.

About this time, my acting teacher started dating a guy in L.A. who was a personal manager that represented kids in the business. After reading a scene with him, he signed me and helped me get an agent in California. Now I was getting submitted for projects in Hollywood. They would submit my resume, head shot, and videotape to casting directors. If they expressed an interest in meeting me, I would fly out at my own expense, but I was always guaranteed a meeting with at least the director.

This is how I landed the part in the television series *Silver Spoons*. Originally, I was only hired for one episode, but the producers liked me and ratings were strong, so they asked me back five more times. It looked as if I were about to become a regular cast member and do several more episodes. They even brought in a guy to play my dad. But it didn't happen.

Silver Spoons was a great experience. We filmed at Universal Studios in front of a live audience. I signed autographs, received fan mail, appeared in *Teen* magazine, and even got nominated for a Youth in Film Award as best new actor in a comedy series. Plus, Embassy Television, the production company that owned *Silver Spoons*, also produced *Diff'rent Strokes, The Facts of Life,* and *One Day at a Time*—the most popular shows on television for several years.

One week I'd been watching these shows in my room, and now, all of a sudden, I was working in the same rehearsal hall with the biggest stars on television.

Socially, my manager and I were playing racquetball with

Ricky Schroder and his bodyguard, as well as with Jason Bateman and his dad. I think most people just let Ricky win, but I was way too competitive for that—it would have never worked. But truth be told, he was pretty good, and his bodyguard was a ringer, so we traded games.

A Moment of Decision

Looking back, it's hard to believe my career got started with just a little faith and determination. But then again, that's how every success starts out. I simply believed that if someone else could do it, then I could too. And I felt that I deserved it just as much as the next guy. This is the exact same message I want to convey to you in this book. I was born with no great advantages; I was just a short, stocky, Irish kid who refused to give up. And if I can do it—so can you!

As my skills improved, my confidence grew, and I began to have some success. Small victories produced bigger ones. Likewise, I had a nothing-ventured, nothing-gained attitude. If I didn't get a part, no big deal—I didn't have it yesterday either, so nothing was lost. I really had no fear of failure, because no one was putting pressure on me—not even myself. I was just having fun and seeing what was possible. This is a very powerful approach to life: to just relax, have fun, and go with the flow.

During my auditions, while other kids were bragging about their agent or all the parts they were about to land, I would go off by myself, learn my lines, and study my character and the scene. I didn't want any distractions. After I felt prepared, I would start getting mentally ready. I'd remind myself of empowering thoughts and build my feelings of certainty about getting the part. Walking through that door, I wanted to be in a peak state of mind and "feeling." This method proved to be very effective and was one of the big reasons my success rate was uncommonly high.

Using this technique, my feelings of faith grew strong; I just assumed that I would get every part. After *Silver Spoons*, for example, I read for a role in the major feature film from Paramount Pictures called *Explorers*. I remember walking into the director's office, doing my scene, and thinking, *Well, when do I start?*

I wasn't being arrogant; I had just become very self-assured. I mean, why would I fly all the way to L.A. and not get the job? That just made no sense. Paramount probably read every kid from L.A. to New York for that role, and my meeting lasted about five minutes. But I got the job.

This highly anticipated, $30 million movie was projected to be the next *E.T.* Joe Dante, one of the hottest directors in Hollywood, directed the movie. He had just finished *Gremlins*, a huge box-office success. The movie starred Ethan Hawke, who was later nominated for an Academy Award in *Training Day*, and River Phoenix from *Stand By Me*.

Unfortunately, the production company decided to cut the last 20 percent of the script and a sequence of special effects. The results were not favorable; the movie did not meet up to the huge expectations. Nor did it launch my career to the next level, as anticipated.

By this time, I was sixteen and a half—a challenging age for teenage actors, especially those living outside Los Angles. Movie companies prefer to hire actors who are eighteen to play younger kids. It saves the studios millions of dollars, because then they don't have to be restricted by child labor laws. Once you are legally an adult, they can work you for much longer hours and don't have to pay for a tutor.

I had a decision to make. I could split up my family and move my mom and myself to California, in hopes of getting some work during this tricky time. Or I could stay in Texas, graduate with all my friends, and move to California by myself at eighteen. Ultimately, I decided to be a normal kid. I figured I had my whole life to be an actor, but I'd never be able to go back and relive my senior year of high school. Friends, girls, and sports won out.

After all, I was sixteen.

Reality Check

As a teenager, I had risen from humble earnings of $20 a week mowing the family lawn to $3,500 per week as a TV actor. But the real money was all around me, just beyond my reach. Working among teenagers and adults making in excess of $25,000 a week, it appeared my payday was coming soon.

Feeling destined for fortune and fame, I packed my bags and headed for Hollywood just days after high school graduation. Expectations for my adult career were lofty, given my rare success as a teenager. However, the highest ambitions were my own. I fully intended to be a millionaire by twenty-one, appearing on a hit television show and living in Malibu, with a black Porsche 911 perched in the driveway.

Reaching the sun-drenched beaches of California, feeling the cool ocean breeze, and watching the waves crash confirmed my thoughts of destiny. I was totally free—thousands of miles from home, some cash in the bank and with my first apartment. Looking at the privileged lifestyle of Malibu residents, with their fashionable beachfront homes and spectacular coastal views, I felt certain that we would soon be neighbors.

After getting settled, I called up Jason Bateman, one of my old chums from *Silver Spoons*. He had recently moved into his own place, and he invited me over to check it out. Entering his stylish new pad, it was immediately clear that he was tasting the good life of show business. His starter home was a luxury townhome near the beach.

Jason had landed a TV series after *Silver Spoons* and was currently working on a project. We caught up for a bit, and then he grabbed two sets of keys, saying he wanted to show me his new wheels. We descended into the garage to find a luxury SUV and a Porsche 911. I couldn't believe it; he was only eighteen.

I always knew Jason would be successful; he was one of those kids in the business who always worked. He was a talented actor, but more important, he knew how to turn on the charm and get the job. Intoxicated by the feeling that really expensive stuff gives you, I left his place hoping my time was coming soon.

A highly personal example of young success, this scene was clear evidence that it could happen to me. Likewise, River Phoenix, whom I worked with in the movie *Explorers,* was doing extremely well—a reality that further fueled my ambition and expectation of success. I started to put more pressure on myself to succeed.

One of the unique aspects of show business is the fact that if you land the right role in a TV series or major movie, you can make your personal fortune in a relatively short period of time—a fact that many actors can't help always having in the back of their mind. But it rarely happens that way . . .

My dreams soon collided with some sobering realities and tough setbacks that dimmed the neon lights of Hollywood. Having moved to L.A. so early in the summer, it was a long time before college was to start. I'd left my friends, family, and girlfriend behind and didn't have any real friends. My manager and I had been close at one time, but our relationship had become primarily about the business.

Alone in a city not exactly known for its hospitality, I suddenly had no social life whatsoever. I met a few people at my apartment, but no one I would call a friend. Most weekends I had no plans at all; it got really lonely. I wasn't used to having no social life, and I didn't like it.

Plus, I wasn't getting many auditions, and even fewer good ones. I'd dreamed of this time in my life for years, and now nothing was happening. I started to get restless. Waiting for the phone to ring is one of the toughest aspects of being an out-of-work actor; it wears on you. The pressure of my huge expectations, the success of my previous coworkers, and the massive displays of wealth in California began to take their toll on me.

Likewise, it quickly became apparent that the eighteen months I'd taken off to graduate high school was equal to about ten years in Hollywood time. Casting directors want to know what you've done lately. I was no longer riding the momentum of previous projects. Once a hot commodity, now I was just an actor who hadn't worked in the last couple years.

Finally, the long summer ended, and my first semester began at Cal State, Northridge—a school where it became apparent that if you wanted any kind of social life, pledging a fraternity was the way to go. Fortunately, I met an exceptional group of guys and pledged Pi Kappa Alpha.

My life immediately changed. Surrounded by admired leaders who called me brother (which had very strong appeal for me as an only child), there were cute girls everywhere, and blowout parties. I was well respected on campus, and I had a real life again—a great life.

I started to relax and regain some balance. My auditions got better, and I landed an episode on a TV show. Then I made callbacks multiple times for the lead in a TV series called *Growing Pains*, a show that ended up running for many years. Landing this role would have changed the game. Close, but no cigar.

Unfortunately, my manager thought that my fraternity was just one big party and my career was not my first priority. It was much deeper than that for me; my fraternity brothers had become my family. I developed friendships among that group and created memories that I still cherish today. But my manager didn't understand the true depth of these friendships and he soon decided to end our relationship.

Representation is extremely important in the entertainment industry; this incident was a damaging blow to my career and me. Never having realized the full value of his efforts, because many of them had been behind-the-scenes, I definitely felt the effects once he was gone. He had helped get my foot in the door for the right projects and had been my experienced adviser in a tough business, but more important, at one time, he had been my close friend.

I discovered another reason that the quality of my auditions had declined. My agent was great for actors ages fourteen to sixteen, but he was not really known for talent in my current age group. This was limiting my opportunities to read for certain projects. Realizing the situation, I tried to get a new agent, but it was difficult because I hadn't done anything major in the last couple years.

Caught in a very frustrating catch-22, it just wasn't fun anymore. You must love what you do to be successful in the entertainment business—and I got to the point that I didn't love it any longer.

Determined to make a comeback in terms of my self-esteem, I decided to pursue another area of interest: the real estate business. At the time, several real estate gurus were endorsing buying and fixing up foreclosures with little or no money down. This was attractive since I had little to no money left.

When I attended a seminar in L.A., many references were made to the opportunities in Texas. Given my interest in real estate, my strong desire to be self-employed, and my limited capital, it seemed like a good fit. Convinced that this was a golden opportunity, I gambled the last of my savings and signed up for a special three-day event in Hawaii called the Millionaires School.

Returning home to Texas, I quickly learned it wasn't as easy as it sounded. I bought a few homes, made improvements, and tried to flip them for a profit. I was certainly ambitious enough, but I lacked experience. A few rookie mistakes cost me several thousand dollars, which seemed like a million at the time.

So there I stood, my dreams of a successful acting career had failed, my dreams of being a wealthy real estate investor had failed, and I was up to my eyeballs in debt for the first time in my life. I had no job and no college degree, and I'd blown through all my savings. While my college friends were graduating, getting good jobs, and starting companies, I was forced to move back in with my parents.

But the most painful part was the fact that I felt like a complete failure. My sense of self-worth was deeply wounded. Bruised, battered, and broken, I spiraled into devastating depression that would last more than a year.

Turning Point

Sometimes there's a greater reason *our plans* don't work out, but we can't see it at the time. Often, our biggest disappointments end up being huge blessings. During the early stages of my transformation, while I was living back at home with my folks, this truth was revealed to me in a very personal and profound way.

One morning, I was sitting at the breakfast table when my mom plopped my new *Time* magazine down in front of me. River Phoenix, whom I had worked with in the movie *Explorers*, was on the cover. He had died of a drug overdose outside the Viper Room, a hip Hollywood club partly owned by Johnny Depp.

Seeing River's face on the cover haunted me—it was like looking in a mirror. The photo looked identical to one of my old head shots. River and I were about the same age and had a very similar look. In fact, as teenagers, we had constantly competed against one another for acting parts.

As I sat stunned at the kitchen table, a warm presence washed over my entire body, like a wave of intense calm. I *heard* a faint inner voice, letting me know this was the reason my career had not continued. I was still too young, too wild, and too reckless. Had I gotten everything I wanted at such a young age, it would have ended in disaster.

An image appeared in my mind: I was driving a Porsche 911 Carrera, racing through a winding canyon road. It was early morning, maybe three or four a.m., and there was an attractive girl in the passenger seat. We were on our way home after a late-night party when suddenly, we took a curve too fast and broke through the guardrail, plunging into the canyon below.

The warm presence then faded away, and I sat there in majestic silence for several minutes. I emerged knowing I had heard a divine voice, knowing he was right, and knowing he was preparing me for something else—redirecting my path.

A New Journey Begins

While my acting career was exciting, it does not compare to the thrills of my authentic spiritual journey. This voyage has produced the most profound moments of my life and propelled me into a far superior adventure. *Pursuing the path of spiritual growth described in this book was the wisest decision I ever made; by redirecting my faith, desire, and persistence to these principles, I transformed my life.*

As a kid, spirituality was never presented in a way that inspired me, so I sought my thrills elsewhere. Mentors always seemed to be telling me what to do or hitting me up for money. I felt more restricted than inspired.

Later, I would learn that God does not seek to control us; he simply wants us to develop strong character, to do the "right" thing, and to treat our fellow man with kindness, fairness, and respect. He does not seek to confine us; he allows each soul to develop in its own way. It's not about giving up our individual personality; it's about becoming the person we were created to be. The essence of true spirituality is simply friendship with God and striving to further a feeling of brotherhood in our world.

It is my great joy to share with you in the coming pages the principles that transformed my pain and suffering into a life of profound and real satisfaction. Now that's a true Hollywood story.

2
SHIFT HAPPENS

I conceive that the great part of the miseries of mankind are brought upon them by false estimates they have made of the value of things.

—BENJAMIN FRANKLIN

Some of my toughest life lessons and most liberating personal victories have been related to money. By sharing my life experiences and the insights gained, I hope to help you avoid these painful lessons, develop a balanced perspective on money, and achieve greater prosperity in all areas of your life.

In this chapter, my story continues. I want to share with you what I learned about the lure of materialism; about how there are no shortcuts to success—even though we want to believe there are; about facing financial adversity; and about the important mental shifts that occurred to help me create financial prosperity and understand the true meaning of success.

The Lure of Materialism

Materialism has reached epic heights within the neon glow of our entertainment-based society. Huge salaries of celebrities and professional athletes are constant fascinations. Lavish lifestyles and vast personal fortunes are regular attractions on TV and through the front windshields of Americans. These ever-present temptations seep into the psyche of millions and exert a strong, steady, seductive pull.

Materialism is perhaps one of the biggest problems facing our society, and its ripple effects can be devastating. Money is just ink on paper; but it's the source of immeasurable stress and personal pain; destroying countless marriages, friendships, and lives. When combined with the relentless desire to succeed in America and our expectation of immediate gratification, the love of money can be deadly. In fact, as you read in the first chapter, these temptations took me to the brink of suicide as a young adult.

The lure of money is so dangerous today because it's become so beautiful, so ingenious, and so deeply ingrained in our culture. Advertising has become an art-form, crafted by highly creative minds to evoke our strongest human desires. Products are sleeker, sexier, and more alluring than ever, and they're endorsed by the most persuasive, influential people on the planet.

Our ego-driven economy stokes the fire of human ambition by defining *success* as the ownership of fine luxury goods—the trophies of material wealth. Advertisers assure us that trading our money for their wares will make us feel better, happier, and more peaceful. Members of society who are intoxicated by this influence further endorse this message.

These subtle yet potent messages confuse many people's perception of money and lead them to pursue happiness and self-worth through the conquest of earthly ambitions and the accumulation of material possessions. But like any good buzz, it wears off—the effects are only temporary and produce limited satisfaction.

If we remain under materialism's spell too long, we can awaken to find that our life has been reduced to an endless cycle of acquisitions. When this happens, we are destined to find emptiness and feel disconnected from the deepest part of ourselves. Because the deep satisfactions we crave—true happiness, lasting peace, and genuine self-worth—are not commodities for sale. We cannot feed our souls with material things.

Now, I'm not suggesting that making money is unimportant. It's certainly a practical aspect of living that can enhance our quality of life. I'm saying that it's essential we get money in proper perspective and manage it wisely, so we can create happy, well-balanced lives. Prosperity can be achieved without experiencing the harmful personal effects of materialism.

> *It is a preoccupation with possessions,*
> *more than anything else, that prevents us*
> *from living freely and nobly.*
> —BERTRAND RUSSELL

No Shortcuts to Success

In our fast-paced, competitive world, *it's imperative we realize that ambition is a double-edged sword.* While ambition is very helpful in the pursuit of our dreams, it can get out of balance and cause serious problems. My youthful desire for wealth and success led me to put incredible amounts of pressure on myself, making it far more difficult to succeed. Carrying the burden of massive expectations drains our energy and makes life a chore. Anything less than huge success we see as a personal failure. I became a slave to my ambitions, and it made me miserable.

As an adult who's gained years of life experience, I realize that my youthful notions were a bit idealistic. However, the potency of this message is highly relevant to millions of adults in our aggressive world: *If our yearning for money and career success becomes the dominant drive in our life, it can lead to some intense personal pain.* And with the pressures of the American workplace combined with significant financial overhead and the widespread cultural influences of materialism, it's easy to lose equilibrium.

If we remain in this unbalanced state, we ultimately arise one morning feeling lost, confused, and unfulfilled—disconnected from our true self. And that's not a good place to be. Unbridled ambition can completely blind us to our deeper spiritual needs. Our souls cannot be fed by the conquest of material goals. We need quality spiritual food and a method of spiritual growth that inspires us. Our earthly aspirations are healthiest when they are balanced out by spirituality, love, friendship, laughter, and good times.

My next giant mistake was placing too much of my self-worth in my career. *Deriving an excessive amount of our self-value from what we do for a living or a particular skill is a very dangerous proposition.* And it's easy to do because making a living is such an integral part of life.

But what happens if the tides of adversity take our career away? Like having a beachfront home swept out to sea, we are left with nothing, only personal pain. Acting made me feel special, unique, and different; it brought me money, popularity, and attention from beautiful girls. It wasn't easy when it faded away.

We should never put ourselves in such a vulnerable position. It's far wiser to build our self-worth on the solid foundation of personal integrity, noble character, and honorable living.

Here's another essential truth I realized: *there are no shortcuts to success!* In our immediate gratification society, we expect everything to happen quickly, but it takes *time* to create prosperity. Ambition and a positive attitude are important, but *experience is priceless*. It's true, there really is no business like show business—I couldn't find any that were producing eighteen-year-olds driving Porsches.

In the entertainment business, you *can* get rich quick, but it rarely happens that way. Typically, it happens over years of intense struggle, working odd jobs, perfecting your craft, and finally catching a break. Al Pacino performed on stage in New York for ten years, making $200 a week, before appearing in *The Godfather*. Harrison Ford worked as a carpenter for years before he had success in films. Clint Eastwood worked at a gas station and dug swimming pools, and even when he finally landed a part in a TV series, he was locked into a studio contract for seven years, not making any real money.

While my experiences in the entertainment industry were first-hand, television, the news media, the Internet, and social media exert the same powerful influence on millions of young people and adults in our world. Entertainers like Britney Spears, Justin Timberlake, Ashton Kutcher, Katy Perry, and Miley Cyrus are examples of young wealth and success. *American Idol, The Voice,* and *America's Got Talent* let you know that you can be a star if you are good enough, talented enough, and want it badly enough. *The Apprentice* conveys that you can be rich like Donald Trump if you are smart enough or cunning enough to play the game of life.

The Internet, smartphones, and smart TVs constantly satisfy our craving for instant gratification and reinforce our expectation of rapid results. Our on-demand lifestyle delivers a vast array of products to us with lightning speed. Technology and UPS deliver the entire world to our doorstep. We no longer have to go to the post office, video store, music store, bookstore, movie theater, mall, or restaurant. We just touch a button, and things magically appear; the world is literally in the palm of our hand.

So why should we have to wait for prosperity? *Isn't there an app that can speed this process up?*

Hey, I love technology, but *human* progress isn't that fast. Many times when success doesn't come as soon as expected, we end up questioning ourselves. What did I do wrong? What's wrong with me? Am I not smart enough, good enough, etc.? No, you just aren't there yet.

Sometimes our plans don't work out because we aren't on the right path, a lesson that I will never forget after seeing the picture of River Phoenix on the cover of *Time* magazine. We can't always see the big picture, and we don't always comprehend our lessons right away.

But if we ask for clarity, the answers will eventually come. Maybe not right when we want them, but at a time of greater objectivity, when we can discern the lesson more clearly.

We are afraid that by letting God direct our life, we will end up somewhere we don't want to be or doing something we don't want to do. But in my experience, *it's been exactly the opposite.* Because he knows us better than anyone, he knows what's in best alignment with our natural gifts and what will bring us optimum satisfaction in life.

Failure is simply to keep repeating the same mistakes—and not gaining wisdom from our experiences. Failure is closing our minds to truth.

Successful people fail their way to success. Walt Disney went bankrupt eight times. Abraham Lincoln suffered many failures and then changed the course of human history.

These monumental life lessons and personal discoveries really helped me to let go of my past mistakes and stop beating myself up about them. We must learn to be patient and kind to ourselves as we acquire knowledge, develop skills, and gain experience. Resources and assets are helpful, but it's truly the person you become on the journey that's most valuable.

Look at a bigger picture; don't be too short-sighted with your goals. Maybe you're just not there yet or on the wrong path. Try to learn from the mistakes of others as much as possible so you don't have to endure needless suffering. Learn to laugh at yourself. This is a huge asset and makes life a lot more fun. My darkest days were those without laughter.

> *Employ your time in improving yourself by other men's writings, so that you shall gain easily what others have labored hard for.*
> —SOCRATES

The Shift

In time, I overcame personal defeat and financial adversity. Ironically, the less I focused on money, the more financial success I experienced. My own prosperity has been the result of discovering key truths about money, making a few important mental shifts, and applying the principles in this book to my profession.

The first crucial shift happened when I started pursuing a path of spiritual growth. In answer to a very sincere prayer, God delivered an important teacher into my life. During our first meeting, she assured me that if I transferred my energy into spirituality and living in harmony with universal principles, I would not only attain financial prosperity but success in all areas of life. Since she had achieved an astonishing level of peace, significant professional success, and a generous six-figure income, I trusted her advice.

This change in mental focus was essential, and it restored

some much-needed balance to my life. Making time for spiritual reflection, I began studying the principles in this book and many others. But more importantly, I started testing these truths in my life and producing fantastic results. I learned how to manage my "estate of mind," become the real me, see the big picture, awaken my spiritual energies, pay attention to signs, do the Greater Good, and handle life's details—every principle I'll share with you in part Two.

Likewise, I made God my business partner, allowing him to guide me and open the right doors—*those meant for me*. I paid attention to and chose the paths that flowed smoothly, while avoiding those fraught with roadblocks, knowing this was not his way.

We must realize that God wants us to prosper; the universe wants us to succeed. He always wants what's best for us; we must learn to let go and let God. But it's a *partnership,* which means we must work together and do our part. We need to handle our details, make greater-good decisions, and pay attention to the signs he shows us. He just doesn't want us to become so consumed by material things that we ignore him and neglect the progress of our soul.

Prosperity achieved by spiritual living is distinctly different from a mind-set of wealth derived through extreme ambition. *Prosperity* can be defined as a state of financial well-being in which you have what you need and then some—a surplus. You are comfortable and have reserves. Obviously, there are different levels of abundance, but the mind-set is essentially the same. You have plenty but aren't consumed by money or material things.

In contrast, a mind dominated by *excessive* thoughts of money or material possessions crosses a *mental border* into the realm of materialism. A state of infatuation or the "love of money" is often characterized by consumption that's extreme, unnecessary, or wasteful. Purchases are often motivated by ego, prestige, or the desire to impress others.

As important changes took hold in my life and I began to spiritualize my thinking, God introduced me to a real, live millionaire—a man who just happened to be the most miserable person I'd ever met. At first, I was completely unaware of his financial situation. I just saw a very sad, lonely man. But in our dealings, he revealed that he'd started his own company and at one point had $10 million in the bank.

Fascinated by the prospect of having so much money, I asked him how it felt—and I'll never forget his answer. He said, "Son, no matter how much money I made, it was never enough—I only wanted more."

Stunned by the magnitude of this statement, its meaning slowly penetrated my skull. Making millions of dollars hadn't brought him peace, happiness, or real satisfaction—all the things I once thought it would do for me. Wow, I could have done all that work and still not gotten what I wanted. It was truly a life-altering moment.

Then I caught a TV special on the *Mega Rich in America*. The reporter was interviewing a wealthy hedge fund manager on Wall Street, whose net worth was $75 million. When the journalist asked if he was content, the guy said, "Not yet." Buddy, go play some golf, take your girlfriend to dinner, and relax. Another glaring example of a colossal truth: *if our goals are only materialistic pursuits, we will never be satisfied.*

Facing Adversity

Let's return to my story, the part where everything had fallen apart and I'd moved back home with my parents. Never in my wildest dreams could I have imagined that by my early twenties, my confidence and feelings of self-worth would be so damaged that I no longer even recognized myself. I was no longer strong enough to act on my desires. These feelings had to be completely rebuilt, reconstructed from a very difficult place within myself, like the buildings of a war-torn country.

During this early phase of my growth, I worked two jobs to pay off my debts, got my real estate license, and eventually moved back into my own place. Then I met a broker I liked who specialized in leasing luxury apartments, townhomes, and condos in an upscale part of town. An entrepreneur at heart, and still determined to be self-employed, I saved a few thousand dollars and joined his firm.

My first year started off well. I really enjoyed having my own business, working from home, setting my own schedule, and answering ad calls by the pool. I was having fun and making money—not big money, but I treasured the freedom of my lifestyle.

Then I met a girl. Before long, we were engaged, and I was actively involved in helping plan and pay for the wedding, not to mention dealing with the significant drama of a mother terrified of losing her only son. Good times.

Simultaneously, I had past clients who now wanted to buy. But my broker was only structured to handle leases, so I had to turn them away. Not wanting to miss out on future commissions, I decided to expand my services, which meant finding a new broker and office.

Unfortunately, my new broker was a skilled salesperson but not a very good business manager. Realizing his shortcomings, he quickly joined a well-known real estate franchise. However, the transfer was poorly executed and produced a ton of chaos in the office, resulting in half the agents leaving. This upheaval also created a difficult atmosphere for a new agent like me.

After the wedding and a Caribbean honeymoon, we tallied up the damage. We combined her credit card balances with mine, added in the expenses from the wedding and honeymoon, put my self-employment tax bill on top—and I was securely, innocently, youthfully, and quickly back in debt. Given the weight of my responsibilities, my current office situation, and the length of time it took to get paid in real estate, I decided to sacrifice the freedom of owning my own business and get another kind of job.

Shift Happens—Again

In time, I landed a sales position with a high-end furniture company. Determined to learn from my previous mistakes, I dedicated myself to professional development. I learned my craft and business thoroughly, studied top company leaders, developed my skills, and gained precious experience. Likewise, I implemented this book's principles in my business.

In two years, I was ranked as one of the top ten out of more than two hundred sales people in the United States, and I was promoted to manager of a highly sought-after showroom. Located in a wealthy suburb, it was to be the model showroom for the next one hundred stores.

While my young wife and I had eliminated a considerable amount of debt, we hadn't put back any substantial savings yet. We were still living month to month, which creates added stress when you operate on straight commission. Working on commission takes faith, and I had come through some difficult financial times, not to mention having dealt with the constant pressure to hit company goals.

God had proven to me over the last couple of years that I

just needed to do my part and he would handle the rest, but I still sometimes struggled with worry about money. Now I had he added responsibilities of running the day-to-day operations of a highly visible million-dollar showroom. I did not want to fail.

Driven by this promotion, I picked up a new book on professional success that led me to make another significant adjustment. The author talked about reaching a point in his career when he had *shifted from a profit motive to a service motive*. This concept fit perfectly with the spiritual principles I'd been studying, and it just clicked. The essence of our spiritual growth means rising above self-interest, getting outside ourselves, and treating others the way we would want to be treated.

Realizing my job was much more enjoyable when I just had fun with my customers and helped them out, and recognizing that worrying about money was a complete waste of time, *I made an irrevocable decision*. Instead of thinking about the money, I was going to shift my focus *totally* to being great at my job and taking care of my customers. My income would be *solely* the result of the quality of my service. I would do my best, and then just let go and let God.

This shift was extremely successful. My income and business flourished, and money continued to lose influence over me. *It's far easier to make money when you don't focus on the money.* I was no longer carrying the weight of its inflated importance.

It's not that I was greedy or didn't care about my customers before this change; people bought from me because they liked me, trusted me, and I gave them good advice. But this shift was very deliberate, focused, and *resolute*.

Later in my career, I landed a job selling houses for Centex Homes, one of the nation's leading home builders. In Dallas/

Fort Worth, their largest and number-one division in the United States, I was competing with some of the best sales professionals in the industry. Many of my new colleagues had fifteen to twenty years' industry experience and had earned seats in prime locations.

My first assignment out of training was a start-up neighborhood on the outskirts of town. Having studied my new business thoroughly, I again implemented this book's principles in my business. My first two years, I sold 221 homes, distinguishing myself among the very best in a highly competitive field. Out of more than eighty top professionals, I was again ranked in the top ten.

Being good at your occupation does offer some satisfaction, and we all must make a living. But these satisfactions have limited depth, for they don't reach the soul level. *Let our professional success be the result of our valuable service to others.*

True Success

I like my material comforts, but I don't seek to define myself by what I own. I'm not looking for my possessions to fulfill me, make me feel better about myself or bring me inner peace. I no longer have the desire to impress or compete with anyone. Material assets are in proper perspective. These days, I try not to love anything that cannot love me back.

The most gratifying feature of prosperity is that it helps us to think about money less and focus on aspects of life that bring us deeper satisfaction. It allows us greater control over our most precious resource: time.

True success is not defined by what we own. It's a collection of moments—moments spent at peace with those we love, experiencing great friendship, laughter, and joy. It's time spent in pursuit of our goals, dreams, and personal life mission—moments spent attuned to the presence of God, experiencing insight. We cannot feed our soul by the conquest of earthly ambitions or the accumulation of material possessions. Our soul transcends this world, while the stuff stays here.

> *The price of anything is the amount of life you exchange for it.*
> —HENRY DAVID THOREAU

PART TWO

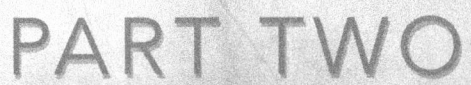

7 PRINCIPLES FOR SUCCESSFUL LIVING

3

MANAGE YOUR ESTATE OF MIND

You are a product of all of the the thoughts you have thought, feelings you have felt, and actions you have taken up until now. And . . . the thoughts you think today, feelings you feel today, and actions you take today will determine your experiences tomorrow.

—JACK CANFIELD

The first principle I want to share with you deals with a unique piece of real estate. What if you were given a beautiful mansion nestled atop the rugged hills of the California coastline? Imagine diving into your infinity pool and emerging at the water's edge. Gazing upon the Pacific, a feeling of complete freedom overwhelms you. You can become anyone you want and create any life you choose.

Well, we all have such a place: our mind.

Our Estate of Mind is the most important place on earth. This mental mansion is the most valuable piece of real estate we will ever own—our true home. It's here we shape our destiny, determine our self-concept, and create our life from the inside out. No matter how far we travel in this world, we will always live in our mind.

Managing our Estate of Mind, keeping its contents positive, should be our most important priority. We need to take great care in the thoughts we allow to inhabit this precious space. Likewise, we need to proactively fill it with positive material: our hopes, dreams, goals, affirmative thoughts about ourselves, high-quality intellectual and spiritual food, uplifting stories, inspirational quotes, areas of interest, enjoyable activities, exciting projects, future travel plans, and humor.

But we get so busy dealing with our obligations that we lose sight of this crucial perspective. Life pulls us in so many directions that we don't take care of ourselves in this very important way. We're so busy paying the mortgage, raising children, doing household chores, staying in shape, and getting the oil changed that we sometimes neglect our greatest responsibility. It's easy to get complacent and linger in undesirable mental places.

In this chapter, we will look at why managing our Estate of Mind is so important. We'll also explore two significant ways to make sure our mind is a place and source of positivity: living in the now and having a goal we feel passionate about.

Why a Positive Estate of Mind is Important

Maintaining a positive Estate of Mind is critical because our thoughts determine the life we create. Human beings are like guided missiles—our repeated thoughts set the coordinates that determine our path and where we ultimately land. We are truly masters of our own destiny.

Our thoughts send out electrical impulses, or vibrations, throughout our body and also permeate the space around us. Our thoughts affect our *inner state of being*—reflected in how we feel, the words we speak, the tone and inflection of our voice, our facial expressions, our body language, and ultimately, our actions, or outer behavior.

People pick up on the energy we send out, and they respond to it instinctively. For example, comedian Will Ferrell can walk onstage and literally change the atmosphere in the room. He exudes a charm and childlike enthusiasm that's infectious. People love him because they are uplifted by his presence. He's a huge star but just a big kid at heart, reminding us not to take ourselves too seriously.

The more times we repeat a given thought, the stronger the signal we emit. The receptivity of others is influenced by their own inner condition, what they have going on in their mind and body, and how mentally present they are.

When we're in a positive state, we attract good things and people into our lives. We create opportunities, handle situations more skillfully, produce better results, and impact others in an uplifting way. Positive people love to be around this powerful energy; they sense it, feel it, and gravitate toward it. This human gravity has been called The Law of Attraction and has been the subject of several popular books, including *The Secret* by Rhonda Byrne and *Jack Canfield's Key to Living the Law of Attraction*.

In essence, this law states that like attracts like. When we drift into a negative mental state, we attract more negativity. We tend to be more emotional, less objective, and unable to handle situations well. We end up making things worse and causing problems for others and ourselves. Negativity stirs up more negativity.

Have you ever known someone who was so toxic that you just felt bad being around him or her? I once worked with a realtor who was so pessimistic that she would talk her clients out of a great home once they fell in love with it.

Anger is another example; it creates a path of destruction. Like the wake of a boat, it causes a ripple effect. It's important that the ripples radiating out from us be life enhancing rather than life damaging. More on this in the next chapter.

Living in the Now

Let's look now at two of the most powerful ways to create and maintain a positive Estate of Mind.

The first is *learning to live in the NOW*. This principle sounds simple, but the results we achieve by living this way are HUGE. So much of the suffering we experience in life results from residing either in the future or in the past—anywhere but here, now. Developing the habit of living in the now significantly improves our quality of life and simplifies the task of managing our minds.

Years ago, I heard a statistic that absolutely stunned me: 97 percent of the things we worry about never actually happen. People spend countless hours worrying about future events that never come. We imagine these scenarios that create confusion and generate untold stress for nothing. What an enormous waste of time and energy. Repulsed by this practice, I regularly remind myself of this fact to keep myself from slipping into this trap.

The events of the weekend before my wife and I were supposed to close on our new home provide a great example of avoiding this pitfall. We'd been living in a hotel with our two large dogs for three months after selling our previous home. It was Friday afternoon, and our loan was in final review so we could close the following week. I flipped the TV on to CNN, which was reporting breaking news: our country was on the verge of an economic collapse. They were comparing this financial meltdown, brought on by a housing and mortgage crisis, to the Great Depression. All members of Congress were headed to Washington, and nobody was going home until a bailout strategy was in place.

I could have stressed out about it all weekend and frantically watched CNN as I contemplated our fate. Not only was our loan up for final approval, but I was also a straight commission salesperson in the housing industry. It was a perfect storm that could've prevented us from moving into our dream home. But there was absolutely nothing I could do about it. Congress was behind closed doors, and our mortgage company was closed till Monday.

So I figured we should just relax, go out for Mexican food and margaritas, and watch some football on Sunday. This plan turned out to be pretty solid, because interest rates dropped a half percent on Monday; we locked in our rate and closed on the house later in the week.

We must stop trying to manipulate situations and outcomes—certain things in life are simply beyond our control. When faced with a challenging situation, all we can do is strive to live in harmony with universal principles and natural spiritual laws, such as handling our details and making decisions based on the Greater Good. Then, let go of it! Allow God and the universe to handle the rest.

Sometimes when things don't work out the way we hoped, it's simply God redirecting our path. We don't always see the full picture, but he sees every facet of the situation.

On the flip side is the past. Living in the past is not only a colossal waste of time, but it's also perhaps our biggest mistake. Yesterday is gone forever—we can't change what has happened. Dwelling on negative memories only stirs up negativity within us. Replaying these events in our mind evokes the same negative feelings and emotions we experienced at the time. We are essentially reliving these experiences within our mind and body.

If this develops into a habit, it can become a serious problem. This destructive practice is the main reason my depression reached such a critical state. I was so busy trying to figure out why my acting career hadn't panned out that I got stuck living in the past, contemplating where I'd done wrong or what could have been. We must stop dragging the past around with us if we expect to create a happy life. We all make mistakes; just learn from them and move on.

We re-create our lives and ourselves every day. Each morning is a fresh start, a blank canvas on which to craft an engaging life. Living from the viewpoint that each day is "the first day of the rest of our life" is a powerful perspective. Applying this motto was the first step in my personal recovery, and it's an essential component of managing our mind.

Life is simply a series of moments; it's here, in the moment, that everything happens. Either we're living in the moment or we're missing out on life. Residing in the past and agonizing about the future is not really living— it's just going through the motions.

A successful life is a collection of positive days, each day being a *mini-lifetime*. So let's make exciting plans for the future, learn from the past, but strive to always live in the moment.

> **Life is a journey, not a destination.**
> —RALPH WALDO EMERSON

Dreams and Goals

A second powerful and important aspect of maintaining a positive Estate of Mind is *occupying it with a dream or goal that excites us.* This technique has a clarifying and stimulating effect. It gives us a sense of direction so we don't feel as if we're wandering aimlessly through life. Goals propel us forward and help us stay motivated. We produce far more positive energy and exhibit much better control of our mind when we are moving forward, rather than sitting idle. As Napoleon Hill said, "The most practical of all methods for controlling the mind is the habit of keeping it busy with a definite purpose, backed by a definite plan."

Progressive creatures by design, we are meant to get better each day, not sit around with nothing to do. Consistent idleness leads to mental laziness, while productivity makes us feel good about ourselves. Just like a Ferrari, we are meant to be driven. Goals give our life a sense of purpose, direction, and meaning.

Instinctively, we know these vital truths, but it's not enough to merely comprehend them—we must live them. While these principles are not new, they are realities of monumental importance. Let the picture of a stunning seaside abode serve as a constant reminder of the cornerstone truth it represents. Let us etch the slogan "Manage Your Estate of Mind" on our hearts, so it becomes an effective mental cue that helps us achieve our purpose. Let's allow this beautiful coastal home to depict the mental lodging we seek to acquire and preserve.

> *Knowing is not enough; we must apply.*
> *Willing is not enough; we must do....*
> —JOHANN WOLFGANG VON GOETHE

4

BE THE REAL YOU

Our second principle for better living is rediscovering the "real you." Isn't it ironic that people travel the globe trying to find themselves, yet they're constantly in their own company? Many individuals struggle to find peace and simply be themselves, when you'd think this would be so easy. This reality is clear evidence that our inner world can be a confusing place, and this is especially true during times of adversity.

Why do we find it difficult to see ourselves clearly? Why is it such a challenge to live by the mantra "Relax, be yourself, and enjoy life"? You would think that being a positive, happy person who feels good and goes with the flow of life would be our most natural state. However, millions of people in our world are in a state of dis-ease and feel disconnected from their true self. And much of human striving is motivated by the desire to feel better and experience more peace.

The purpose of this chapter is to empower you with valuable insight and practical techniques to help you be at PEACE far more often, resulting in a stronger, more positive, more balanced personality that allows you to feel a deeper connection to who you really are: the Real You. We'll talk about the importance of recognizing, accepting, and expressing our true gifts;

society's influence on the way we see ourselves; how to identify and modify fears and insecurities that stop us from being who we really are; what fear really is; and finally, the essence of self-transformation.

Our Unique Attributes

We are born into this world with a unique collection of human traits, talents, and attributes that lie at the core of our being. One of the greatest satisfactions we can experience is to discover, align with, and express these natural gifts. These positive core aspects of self, our natural tendencies, are the essence of our true personality. They are meant to flow smoothly, like a pure mountain stream.

Given that these foundational elements are positive, we are more fully aligned with them when we reside in a positive state of well-being, both thinking and feeling. Likewise, by remaining in this positive state, we feel a deeper connection to who we really are—our true self.

We should seek to discover and express these distinctive qualities in a way that gives us great joy and that inevitably benefits the lives of others. In this way, we make our unique contribution to this world—simply by being ourselves. Our God-given attributes are valuable resources in helping us craft our best lives.

At the end of the chapter, I will share some strategies to help you uncover these hidden talents, abilities, and interests.

Influences of an Imperfect World

The world we are delivered into is hardly perfect. We encounter a variety of negative influences, imperfect people, and confusing messages as we develop our self-concept. These adverse conditions can produce the internal obstacles of fear and insecurity, which muddy the waters of our true self.

In a perfect world, we would all be raised in peaceful, loving, and stable homes. Parents and family members would support, encourage, and strengthen one another, rather than engage in criticism, antagonism, and conflict. Individuals would realize that these negative behaviors hinder personality growth instead of reinforcing it, and they would therefore cease to act this way.

Likewise, in a perfect world, the vast majority of the people in society would strive to help each other and promote a feeling of human brotherhood. But this is not always the case. There are some fantastic people in this world, but there are still many in a state of imperfection. It's typically a mixed bag; all of us have to deal with a variety of positive and negative influences.

Some of our parents were raised in a generation that endured difficult circumstances: world war, economic depression, violence, racial prejudice, and social injustice. These conditions conveyed the message that the world was a tough place, and, if they wanted to compete, they had better toughen up too.

As a result, they might have passed on their fears and biased viewpoints to us; like physical characteristics, *we can actually inherit them*. For example, parents might transfer their concerns for financial security, influencing their kids to choose more conservative jobs rather than follow their true interests. What if Mick Jagger had been effectively persuaded to enroll in the London School of Economics rather than pursue his passion for music? How many lives have been uplifted by the music of the Rolling Stones and all the bands they've inspired?

Wanting us to succeed, our parents can be overly critical of us, because that's how they were raised. However, negative motivation is not the ideal stimulus for creating strong personalities. Courage and character are more effectively achieved through positive means, ideally through inspiration.

Certainly, there are times for parents to be firm with their children, but regular criticism tends to weaken and destabilize a personality, not strengthen and actualize it. Likewise, this pattern can lead individuals to become impatient and excessively critical of themselves, a habit that negatively impacts their growth.

Some people are born into bad situations. Not all parents have their kids' best interests at heart, and subject their kids to neglect, violence, and forms of abuse. These negative influences can also delay children's growth (though they can't prevent it).

Furthermore, our society promotes some confusing messages about the true measure of self-worth. Our fascination with physical beauty and machismo leads many people to question their value in society. The underlying message that physical attributes are of the utmost importance is prominently displayed and heavily advertised. These false images of self-value then permeate the mind-set of countless people, negatively impacting their self-image.

In America, we've created a highly competitive culture that places great significance on financial achievement. Again, the pervasive influence of the media, the entertainment industry, and our economy perpetuate this competitive environment. It's easy to become indoctrinated into the value system of our materially driven world. People feel the pressure to compete and measure up to their peers; they don't want to fail, so they adapt.

In the land of opportunity, only the best will do. Therefore, we tend to judge ourselves by only the highest standards. And while this environment stimulates certain types of achievement, it can generate some harmful personal side effects. Many people silently fear they will not be good enough; it's here that the problem of not knowing who you really are starts.

Identifying Fears and Insecurities

> *Be kind, for everyone you meet is fighting a hard battle.*
> —PHILO

Millions of people struggle with fear and insecurity as they try to compete in our fast-paced, materialistic world. According to IMS Health, a professional services and analytics company serving the health-care sector, in 2011, 71 million people in the United States alone were estimated to have suffered from an anxiety-related condition or from depression. Antidepressant sales now soar past $11 billion annually. Modifying and more effectively dealing with these negative feelings is perhaps the most important skill we can develop.

But first, we have to clearly understand these negative energies, so we know what we're dealing with. An objective viewpoint is extremely valuable in recognizing their influence and modifying them. It's a perspective that can often be difficult to obtain, though, because our egos try to shield us from the effects of such negative energies.

Fear and insecurity are two sides of the same coin. We can have a regular fear, such as fear of flying, or an insecurity, which is a fear that we are not good enough in some way—in terms of being smart, attractive, rich, thin, tall, tough, young, talented, etc. Insecurity is always directly related to our sense of self; it originates in a lack of self-worth. I refer to insecurities as our negative aspects of self, or false selves, because they are inaccurate expressions of who we are. These false selves make us feel disconnected from our true self, which is positive in nature.

The vast majority of our fears are *false perceptions of reality*, as people spend untold hours worrying about events that never occur (see chapter 3). Of course these fears, or false realities, are very real to us when they're active. But they are deceitful allies, intellectual frauds that try to convince us that we are less than we are and that it's OK for them to disrupt our lives. Common fears in our society include fear of abandonment, fear of not being loved, fear of not having enough money, fear of criticism, fear of failure, and fear of violence.

We all carry a certain number of these fears with us; this is our negative emotional baggage. Of course, not every fear develops into a reoccurring problem—just the ones we hold on to and allow to play out repeatedly. Dealing with these negative feelings can be difficult, especially those we've carried for a long time. But the good news is that, for most people, only a couple of fears cause most of their discomfort. When these are modified, quality of life improves significantly.

Every fear starts out in our mind, which is why it's so important that we stay focused on positive aspects of life. As we discussed in chapter 3, when we drift into a negative state of mind, we cultivate the soil where seeds of fear and self-doubt can be planted. If these negative seeds of thought are nurtured and repeated often enough, they can take root and grow into negative feelings of fear and insecurity.

When these fears are functioning, they are like negative

emotional tornadoes that disrupt our peace and positive flow of energy. These negative feelings cause us to feel off, not ourselves, and in a bad mood. If allowed to persist, this negative energy can get lodged in our central nervous system, causing us to feel stuck. Each repetition of thought is like a whirling revolution; the more we repeat the thought of a fear, the more we feel that fear. If we let this activity continue, we will experience major disharmony. In time, it will lead to a depressed state.

Here's a personal story that illustrates this process. My mom grew up in the wake of the Great Depression, the youngest of eight sisters. Money was tight, and like many large families, my mother's family did what they had to do to survive. The Great Depression was a tragedy that instilled fears about money and impacted the self-worth of many good people.

During this time of struggle, my mom developed a feeling that rich people were better than her—an insecurity she carried for so long that I don't even think she could see it anymore. But she would make subtle comments about wealthy people in the community that clearly revealed her feeling of inferiority.

I heard these comments throughout my childhood but didn't think much of it. I told myself that I was going to be rich anyway, so no big deal. However, you'll recall that in my early twenties, I went through some tough financial times and had to move back in with my folks for a while. During this stressful period, I felt like a complete failure, and this insecurity became rooted. My fear grew in strength and became nasty. I was forced to face it regularly as I tried to dig myself out of debt while working on straight commission.

I wasn't always aware of when this fear was functioning. But as my situation improved, I noticed that whenever I was near the wealthy owners of my company, I started to feel very uncomfortable. As I realized what I was dealing with and could see its influence, I got mad. The more I thought about it, the madder I got; this insecurity was ridiculous. Plus, I intended to be promoted into management to reach my financial goals. This meant meeting with the owners far more often.

Determined not to allow this fear to control me and keep me from achieving my goals, I went to work modifying it. Growth sometimes requires that we move outside our comfort zone—and that's exactly what I did.

I am human and imperfect, but I've made significant advancement in the area of self-transformation. Some aspects of myself I've modified altogether, while others I've transformed to a beneficial degree and continue to work on. I guess my selection to write this book proves that if God only used perfect people to effect change in our world, nothing would ever get done.

The Essence of Self-Transformation

Building strong positive feelings of self-worth and staying centered in these powerful feelings is the essence of self-transformation, or changing the way we feel inside. Managing our *state of self*—residing in and getting back to a positive state of *feeling*—is key to this process.

Many times we return to a positive state, but we're not completely sure how we got there. Gaining insight into this process can be extremely valuable. Likewise, we can use practical tools and techniques to help us live in a positive state more often. Knowledge is power.

Self-worth is a sense of knowing who and what we are. We build and strengthen feelings of self-respect by being a person of integrity and character and by striving to live the right way.

The path of spirituality outlined in this book mightily increases our feelings of genuine self-worth because it emphasizes doing the "right" thing, being a loyal friend, treating people with kindness and respect, remaining devoted to our responsibilities, and helping other people. Likewise, we grow these feelings by simply accepting our own self-value and allowing ourselves the freedom to be who we are.

Self-confidence is a faith-generating tool that supports us while we construct the deeper, stronger, and more solid foundation of self-value. It's a technique of self-affirmation that assists us as we develop our skills, take on new challenges, and compete in a challenging environment.

Staying in a positive state of mind is an important aspect of preserving a positive *state of self*. When we fling open the doors of our mind and dwell on negative thoughts, memories or situations, we encourage and permit these negative energies to be stirred. Lingering in undesirable mental places disrupts our sense of peace and well-being. Then, we must go to work on getting rid of these negative feelings and getting back into a positive *feeling*.

Likewise, holding on to negative emotions such as anger, prejudice, and guilt churns up negativity within us. These potent emotions are like high-powered blenders that cut, tear, and wound us internally. Buddha said, "Holding on to anger is like grasping a hot coal with the intent of throwing it at someone else; you are the only one who gets burned."

When I was struggling with depression, I read many self-help books that talked about the "power of positive thinking" and "self-limiting beliefs." They essentially said that by replacing negative thoughts with positive ones, we would soon reprogram our subconscious minds. But many times, this technique didn't seem to work; it didn't make me *feel* any better. Dealing with fears or insecurities that have been become ingrained over time is not always that simple.

Our beliefs are thoughts that rise to the surface of our mind—thoughts we *feel* to be true. Negative thoughts are oftentimes just symptoms of the underlying problem, which is fear or insecurity.

The key to managing our state of self is replacing a negative FEELING with a positive FEELING! Replacing a negative feeling takes more than a *single* thought *impulse,* or even a few thought impulses. A positive feeling is created by a *series* of positive thought *impulses* that grow into a positive *feeling.*

We get "into" a positive feeling by allowing the positive energy generated by our thoughts to saturate our entire body, then staying immersed in this positive energy until the positive feeling is solidified. Then, the negative feeling fades away and we feel better. In the appendix section entitled "The Toolbox," I'll share techniques that will help you accomplish this task

Let's go back to the previous example about my insecurities at work, and I'll show you how I modified one of them.

First, I clearly identified this insecurity as a fear that rich people were better than me. Then I wrote down the thoughts that entered my mind when I felt this way, helping me to recognize this fear as it tried to influence me. Next, I wrote down examples of wealthy individuals who lacked qualities that I admired. And last, I asked for God's help in getting rid of this negative feeling that was creating so much difficulty.

He soon placed an individual in my path who exemplified the absurdity of this insecurity. This person was a high-powered attorney who probably earned about $10 million per year. He was the epitome of the type of man I did not want to be: egotistical, manipulative, and extremely self-centered.

Initially, we got along great. But then he wanted to purchase some furniture for his vacation home in Colorado. Once he decided that I had the product he wanted, he began to show his true colors. Convinced that he was smarter than everyone on the planet, he tried to manipulate every part of the process. He used hardball negotiating techniques, threatening to buy from a competitor. Then he demanded a specific date and time for his out-of-state delivery, even though a third-party company would have to be used—and they would be contending with snow, ice, and steep mountain passes.

His behavior was such a glaring example of the illogical nature of my insecurity that I never forgot it. The idea that he was a better man than me was ludicrous. He clearly lacked strong character, a quality that I highly regarded. In fact, I was so repulsed by his actions that I tactfully chose not to do business with him.

Sometimes, the best deals you do are the ones you don't do. Certain customers are not worth the negativity they create. They monopolize valuable time better spent on quality business, and people who value your help.

In the future, whenever this feeling tried to surface, I would recognize it and remember this experience. Then, I reminded myself of the truth on this subject and used the tools at the end of this chapter to get rid of this feeling. By repeating this process, this insecurity modified and faded away. The relief gained from transforming this fear was well worth the effort. No longer do I have to contain it when it rises; it no longer rises, because I simply don't feel that way anymore.

The idea that having money makes you a better person is completely illogical. Look at Bernie Madoff. On the other hand, there are many prosperous people, like Tom Hanks, who are wonderful. Money is simply not an accurate measure of a person's true worth.

Born with a survival instinct, we often suppress our fears, get tough, and develop our defenses. Ego is a defense mechanism we use to deal with perceived or real threats in our environment. It's like a protective shield we carry into the world to battle for resources and the satisfaction of human desires.

This tough exterior also helps conceal any self-injuries or personal concerns that might be seen as weaknesses. And while this natural defense is serviceable at times, it's a *false ally* in our journey for peace. This shield is a barrier, an obstruction to be chipped away. When a fear or insecurity is removed or modified, a portion of ego goes with it.

In our quest for increasing peace, we are much better served by letting go of our fears, rather than controlling or suppressing them. Like prisoners, we often shackle our fears and allow them to remain in our presence, rather than reforming or releasing them.

The ingredients of our authentic human self are fortified by our strong positive feelings of self-worth. Combined, they form the foundation of our true human self. Negative aspects of self are false expressions of who we are—they muddy the waters of our true self. Residing in a positive state of self, we reveal our true personality and solidify a deeper connection to *the Real Us*.

Ideas and Suggestions for Discovering Attributes of *the Real You*

- Ask for guidance on this subject during meditation and create a journal to write down the insights you receive.
- Pay attention to talents and abilities that seem to come naturally to you.
- Pursue a form of creative self-expression that you enjoy.
- Pay attention to interests that resurface in your mind, especially those not motivated by money (areas of interest that may be hidden or suppressed because they are not seen as profitable).
- Ask yourself: If money were no object in my life, what would I do?

The attributes you become aware of by implementing these suggestions may lead you to an occupation, but they don't have to; they might just bring you joy, personal satisfaction, and fulfillment, or they might benefit the lives of others in some way.

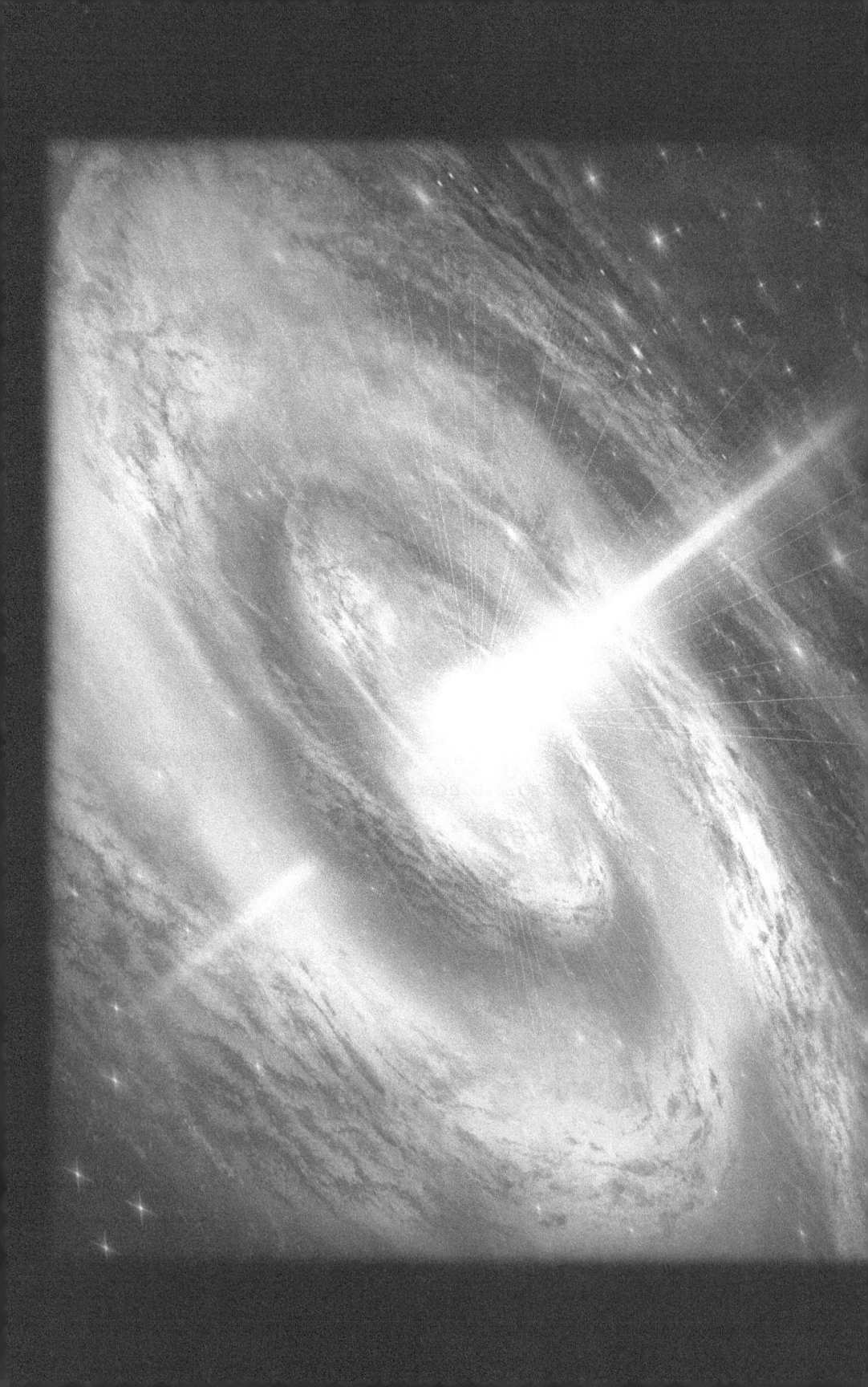

5

SEE THE
BIG PICTURE

*To trust in the force that moves the universe is faith.
Faith isn't blind, it's visionary.
Faith is believing that the universe is on our side
and that the universe knows what it's doing.*

—AUTHOR UNKNOWN

In chapter 3, we talked about having life goals as a key to maintaining a positive Estate of Mind. Having this perspective gives our lives a sense of direction and purpose that's essential in creating our best life. Without worthy goals, we tend to wander aimlessly through life, oftentimes feeling lost, confused, or unhappy. Our finite human minds need a mental structure to function within.

But there's a bigger picture that goes beyond our personal passions: knowing *why we're here* satisfies a deep yearning within us and helps us derive meaning from our life experiences. In this chapter, I'll offer my thoughts on what the true goals of any human life are. Simply stated, they are spiritual in nature:

- To recognize God as our father
- To help promote the brotherhood of all mankind
- To know God as a fact of personal experience and become increasingly like him

In the coming chapters, we'll explore these goals and how to live them. But first, here's a brief introduction to these ideas that gives us "the big picture."

Recognizing God as Our Father

We live in a universe filled with creative activity. The Hubble telescope has captured images, like the one at the beginning of this chapter, that allow us to catch a glimpse of our infinite creator at work—the same divine presence that surges within our souls and seeks to guide us in our personal spiritual journeys. Our short lives on Earth are certainly the very early stages of an endless voyage of spiritual progress and discovery.

The anticipation of a thrilling future beyond this world helps us more cheerfully go about our daily lives, just like the excitement of an upcoming vacation makes it easier to handle a tough week at the office. We greatly benefit from incentives that renew our positive energy. Likewise, a big-picture viewpoint keeps our day-to-day challenges in proper perspective.

Expanding our mind and universalizing our thinking are essential aspects of our progress. How can we ever expect to comprehend an infinite creator if we have a closed mind? We must always remain humble, teachable, and open-minded in our pursuit of growth. Never stop learning, growing, and exploring! We are only scratching the surface of universal intelligence. Only God knows everything.

SEE THE BIG PICTURE

*The only true wisdom is in knowing
you know nothing.*
—SOCRATES

Brotherhood and Spiritual Unity

In the eyes of God, we are all brothers and sisters, all part of the same spiritual family. Like any wise and loving father, he wants his children to get along and help each other. He realizes that we have distinctively different personalities and diverse intellectual opinions, but he also knows we share something much deeper in common.

Every human being in this world has the divine presence of our spiritual father residing within him or her: *the kingdom of God within.* It's the reality of this divine presence that spiritually bonds us all together. The human fraternity of the divine spirit is the essence of spiritual brotherhood. This *universal* message was the heart and soul of the teachings of Jesus.

Of course, we live in a world of immense cultural diversity and passionate individualism. Human beings have an innate desire to express their own uniqueness of being. There will always be diversity of intellectual opinions and personal interpretations of the same divine impulse—but there's no excuse for a lack of spiritual brotherhood. We must focus on the bigger picture: the goals of this life and the human fraternity of the divine spirit. A feeling of spiritual brotherhood must reign supreme in the hearts and minds of all individuals.

Over the years, I've experienced great friendships with some real characters, men and women with strong personalities, adventurous spirits, and independent minds. I've had friends from a variety of religious backgrounds, and my life's been richer for it. As an adult, I have friends who are leaders in their traditional churches and some who feel closest to God in the great outdoors. People's personalities are so different that it's always seemed natural to me that we would have different points of view.

Heck, people order a cup of coffee at Starbucks in a hundred different ways. What makes us think that we could all share the same opinions about an infinite creator? The people who love us, support us, and encourage us are our true family. Friendship is a powerful asset in this life and an open exchange of ideas can be very stimulating.

Personal Spiritual Growth

Spiritual growth means we are evolving the spiritual part of us: our soul. *We generate true soul growth as we become increasingly like God.* We become more like God by increasing our ability to feel his presence, attuning to his plan for our growth, living in harmony with natural spiritual laws, and taking care of life's details. (See chapters 6–9)

Most of our growth is unconscious at first, but as we make progress, we get a deep sense that something has changed—that we have changed. We are still aware of our authentic human self (the personality traits we inherited at birth), but we are definitely different. It's a very exciting shift in our self-awareness. When we become more fully aware of the deep spiritual part of ourselves, we develop greater "soul awareness."

The natural result of spiritual growth is that we begin to display the personal character traits of our divine guide, God. These attributes include increased kindness, fairness, goodness, loyalty, honesty, humility, unselfishness, patience, tolerance, compassion, self-control, happiness, and lasting peace. Exhibiting these qualities in a genuine, unconscious way represents real spiritual progress.

True spirituality is simply friendship with God. The essence of our growth is being a good person, doing the right thing, and living in harmony with natural spiritual laws. It's much easier to make progress when we have clear goals and understand the process. Our life takes on new direction and purpose. We gain experience and acquire wisdom more rapidly. Life becomes more fun because we realize how the game is played.

If we are to be inspired enough to pursue spirituality, it must be presented in a way that makes us want to do it. Early in my life, spiritual growth was not presented in a way that inspired me. The presentation was an inadequate portrayal of what would become the actual experience of knowing God for me.

There are no words that can inspire us like feeling the presence of God. If you are looking for a thrill, look there first.

This is "the big picture"—seeing beyond this earthly stage of our journey, understanding the true spiritual goals of every human, and striving to live them. In the following chapters, I'll share with you specific ways to do this.

6

AWAKEN YOUR SPIRITUAL ENERGIES

> *Deep within man dwell those slumbering powers;*
> *powers that would astonish him, that he never*
> *dreamed of possessing; forces that would revolutionize*
> *his life if aroused and put into action.*
> —ORISON SWETT MARDEN

I've explored many paths in an effort to satisfy my adventurous spirit and my desire for deep satisfaction. I would even go so far as to say I've been a thrill seeker—but honestly, aren't we all just looking for a thrill?

As you know by now, I had many opportunities for thrills early in life. Reaching the heights of prime time television, I got to experience life as a teenage celebrity: fan mail, signing autographs, beautiful groupies, and working with famous people. I tested the rock-star lifestyle: wild parties, adult beverages, and late-night affection. I drove fast cars, jumped motorcycles, rafted Class V whitewater, and flew an airplane solo.

As an adult, I've realized financial prosperity, built my dream home, and traveled to beautiful places.

But nothing has brought me deeper satisfaction or a greater thrill than feeling the presence of God. I believe it is the most exhilarating experience a human can have, and in this chapter, I'll share with you my first spiritual awakening. We'll then explore the essence of true spirituality, the gift of spiritual freedom, and the keys to experiencing the presence of God and moments of spiritual insight.

My First Spiritual Awakening

To be completely honest, growing up, I wasn't even sure there was a God. My parents were not churchgoers, and most Sundays, I'd play football down by the creek. But they were always supportive of me going whenever I expressed an interest. So sometimes I'd spend a Saturday night with a friend and go to church with his family Sunday morning. In Texas, there's a church in every town, so I figured I should check it out.

This gift of spiritual freedom from my parents was an important factor in my growth. It allowed me to develop an open mind toward God and have a genuine experience of the divine from within. Had my parents tried to force their religious views on me, I likely would have rebelled and headed in the other direction. I think most of us have a natural resistance to people telling us what to think; I figured God gave me my own mind, and he expected me to use it.

Attending a variety of churches was interesting, although I admit not all of their theories about God seemed logical to me. I found it fascinating that each group seemed to have a slightly different take on things—yet all were equally convinced they were right. Nevertheless, I went into these experiences with no preconceived ideas about what I was *supposed* to believe and absolutely *no fear* of being wrong. I simply listened to and read the teachings of the various churches I attended with an open mind and a sincere heart.

After church I would go home and reflect on what I'd heard, asking God for his guidance on the subject. I was trying to *tune in* to what felt right—*to see what truth resonated within my soul.* I've always felt that the *spirit* of God, which I felt within me, was my final authority on truth.

Then, one day, it happened. As I was sitting alone in my room, an intense wave of calm washed over me. Every cell in my body began to vibrate at a higher frequency. The entire world seemed to be in harmony, and everything suddenly made complete sense. As I stood up, the room got slightly brighter, as if someone had turned up a dimmer switch. And then the feeling slowly faded . . .

I had felt the peaceful, loving presence of God!

From that moment forward, I could never conceive of God as anything but a loving father. I returned to church with renewed enthusiasm, hoping to experience this feeling again. It had been so pure, authentic, and genuine—and I wanted it badly. But the words I heard only generated a faint glimmer of this powerful experience. While there were a few bright moments in church, most of the time I did not feel inspired, and the routine of going to church without having that experience felt like going through the motions; it did not appeal to my adventurous nature at all.

What I found most disheartening was the fact that many churchgoers *talked* about lofty ideals of living yet weren't *living* them. By Monday, some of them were sitting in judgment of others because they didn't have much money or didn't agree with their religious point of view.

After a while, I just lost interest in going to church. I had learned that God loved me, and that was good enough for me.

I focused my thoughts and energy on the aspects of life I enjoyed most—hanging out with my friends, playing sports, acting, rock 'n' roll, school, and of course, girls. It was not until my early twenties that I began to seek out spirituality in a wholehearted way. It was then that I began pursuing God and paying attention to signs, which I'll share more about in the next chapter.

In the meantime, let me share some thoughts about spirituality and my own beliefs.

The Essence of True Spirituality

There's a rapidly growing trend in our country of people separating themselves from organized religion. A recent survey by the Pew Forum shows that 46 million Americans claim no religious affiliation—the highest number ever. Another 96 million who classify themselves as affiliated say they seldom or never attend church. However, most of these people consider themselves spiritual in some way; many identify themselves as "spiritual but not religious."

A staggering figure like 142 million leads us to ask some thought-provoking questions. And while I find these facts interesting, they simply confirm the changes I've seen taking place in our society. In the last twenty years, I've had several conversations with friends, neighbors, and clients that shed additional light on this development.

So what are the reasons for this dramatic shift in our culture?

What is the essence of true religion? And what does it mean to be spiritual rather than religious?

In our modern world, many people prefer the word *spiritual* to *religious* to describe their *personal relationship with God* and their way of life. A *spiritual* person strives to live rightly, develop strong moral character, and treat his or her fellow humans with kindness, fairness, and respect. He or she seeks enlightenment from a variety of spiritual sources—books, teachers, nature, and meditation—wherever truth is to be found.

A *religious* person also strives to live by strong moral values, altruistic principles, and respect for human dignity. However, he or she is more generally identified with the institution of organized religion and characterized as someone who attends church regularly, adopts a standardized system of beliefs, and seeks truth primarily from traditional doctrine.

In my opinion, individuals tend to define spirituality and religion for themselves, based on their own experiences. Therefore, the meanings of these two terms are sometimes interchangeable. However, I believe *the essence of true spirituality and genuine religion is the same: the personal experience of knowing God*. And true religion is the authentic body of personal experience with this divine reality.

In the Pew survey, individuals overwhelmingly felt that organized religion was focused on the wrong things: rules, money, power, politics, etc.—a fact that my candid conversations with people also uncovered. However, these talks revealed a deeper facet of this new reality: *the people I talked to were simply not inspired by the experience of attending church*.

So what do people really want? Why are they not satisfied? What's at the heart of the matter?

At the core of our being, we desire a connection with God that's too deep for words. This is what we are truly searching for, and when we don't find it, we look somewhere else for something else to fill it. And while there are no words that can excite us like feeling the presence of God, we greatly benefit from an appealing presentation of truth, one that arouses our positive emotions.

Next, we crave a genuine connection with other people. When there's a spiritual element in our relationships, they reach deeper levels. The aspect of social fellowship is a great service that churches provide in our communities. Bringing good people together in a forum of worship helps promote a feeling of spiritual brotherhood that's essential to progress.

Likewise, individuals are clearly expressing their longing for our most precious human freedom: *spiritual liberty.* Asserting their cherished rights of self-expression, they desire to create their own collection of individual truths. They want to lead lives of spiritual originality outside the mental confines of dogma.

Finally, I think this trend of nondenominational spirituality represents a tide of decent people who just want to get along. Deep down, everyone wants to live in a more peaceful world, and many people feel religious labels simply divide mankind. We have seen societies argue and kill each other for centuries in the name of religious views. Perhaps we are starting to see a wave of true spiritual brotherhood that was the cornerstone of Jesus' message.

Look at the products and inventions people love most: the Internet, smartphones, laptops, Facebook, and Twitter, for example. All these innovations allow us incredible personal *freedom* and make it easier to *connect* with others. They make us feel like we are part of a bigger whole. It seems only natural that we would want these same freedoms in our personal spiritual life.

When people become as satisfied with their method of spiritual growth as they are with their smartphones and laptops, we will truly see transformational change in our world. The path of personal spiritual growth presented in this book has been that powerful method for me. This journey has been far more exciting than my iPhone (and I love my iPhone!). I want to give you the iPhone of spirituality, and in my experience, the material in this book is it.

❖ ❖ ❖

In perhaps the greatest teaching of his earthly career, Jesus taught the essence of true spirituality: *the kingdom of God is within*. This monumental declaration swept aside centuries of false belief that God resided far off in the heavens, separate from mankind. Jesus forever made clear that God dwells within us and that true religion is a *personal spiritual experience*.

The kingdom of God within was the cornerstone of Jesus' personal religion—a religion of personal closeness to God, which he taught and demonstrated in his life. The spiritual presence of the father was his authority on all truth, even when it conflicted with the manmade traditions of his day.

Jesus constantly warned Jewish leaders and all humanity not to allow their traditions to distort their own sense of reason. He once healed an afflicted man on the Jewish Sabbath because the man was suffering and needed help—even though this act of kindness and common sense defied the rule perpetuated by the Jewish leaders that the Sabbath was to be a day of rest and that no *work* was to be done. He instructed them not to close their minds to more enlightened teachings. *His faith was not blind; it was visionary.*

When you assemble and illuminate the personal teachings

of Jesus, you see the universal perspective of his message; his core teachings are the heart of the big-picture goals for humans in this lifetime. However, the purity of his message is sometimes obscured by the many teachings about him and reverence for his divine nature.

I've always found it interesting that Jesus did not leave any personal writings behind. Maybe he felt that, upon his departure, individuals would simply divide themselves into separate groups based on their interpretations of his teachings. Likewise, he had already witnessed mankind's tendency to convert written words into rigid rules of living.

Instead, he poured out a highly personal energy to teach us, guide us, and remain ever present. Maybe this spiritual energy was the most fluid and adaptable means of ensuring human progress, helping us to navigate our ever-changing world. Perhaps he felt this *internal river of truth was the best way to help us lead lives of spiritual freedom and originality.*

We are independent spiritual beings who've been given amazing personal resources: the divine spirit of the father (the kingdom of God within—our divine guide), and the spiritual presence of his son (the Spirit of Truth/the Holy Spirit). These versatile teachers are the sources of all truth, the keys to our progress and discovery.

> *I still have many things to tell you, but you can't bear them now. When the Spirit of Truth comes, he will guide you into all truth.*
> —JESUS OF NAZARETH (JOHN 16:12 & 16:13)

Experiencing the Presence of God

God, who is our divine guide, knows us better than anyone.

He knows every facet of our human personality. Therefore, he customizes a plan for our growth that allows our soul to develop in its own unique way. He knows precisely what truth we seek, which experiences we need, and what resources to place in our path. He shows us signs that he personalizes for us, so we will stop and take notice. He is totally dedicated to our spiritual progress.

Yet, whether we invite such spiritual progress is always our decision. Like the dam that controls the flow of a vast river, we control the flow of spiritual resources, often restricting our divine guidance by our lack of cooperation. We gain great benefit by cooperating and being open to growth.

While much of God's work is subtle, hidden from conscious awareness, it is possible to increase our ability to tune in to his presence. Worship is the key to experiencing the kingdom of God within. It is the ideal practice for developing our ability to tap into and attune to his energy.

I'm not talking about worship in the conventional sense of the word—genuine worship is simply taking a feeling of gratitude to deeper levels of love. It has no element of self-interest.

The kingdom of God is a realm deep within us; like in the depths of the ocean, there's a majestic calm. It's a place beyond the rush of daily life, free from emotional conflict and worry. It's an inner place of knowing, where all truth exists. It's where our soul can tune in to its maker. It's a throne of peace, love, acceptance, and humility.

We must make time for spiritual meditation and reflection to have this profound experience. Such practices allow our descent into these deep waters, teaching us how to relax and go slowly. Relaxation is key to this subtle level of understanding. It enhances our ability to resonate with truth. Inner harmony allows us to experience these truths on deeper levels. We need to be open, honest, and teachable like a sincere, truth-seeking child by reminding ourselves that even on our best day, we only comprehend a small portion of God. We must learn to get our ego out of the way—it disrupts the waters.

God tries to reach us in many ways. When he cannot reach us through the inner voice, he seeks to reach us through the voice of others. As God-knowing souls tap into these spiritual energies, truth can be revealed. In this way, we gain insight from the steadfast efforts of others. Seek out teachers who inspire you, those you feel are tapped into these spiritual energies and speak directly to your heart. Look for the spirit of truth in all wise sayings.

When you find truth, don't just comprehend it with your mind—*experience* it with your entire being. *Absorb it—let it saturate your soul.* Feed yourself on the most attractive spiritual food, truth that appeals to your sincere and logical mind and stirs the energies of your soul.

It's in this way that we are truly inspired and build our personal body of truth. The love of God is not a collection of intellectual theories that can be reasoned out in the mind. It's a reality that can only be truly "known" through the fact of *personal experience*. Encountering moments of genuine spiritual insight is thrilling; striving to live more attuned to these energies is our greatest adventure.

In my personal experiences over the last twenty years, I would have to say that God *is* love. And like spirit, love cannot be controlled or contained; it's dynamic and alive. *Love is the most potent state for tuning in to the presence of God.*

7

PAY ATTENTION TO SIGNS

Have you ever dreamed your life could be like a Hollywood movie? Well, it can be—and I'm not exaggerating. You can transform your life into a remarkable journey that has all the thrills of a well-directed, well-cast movie when you pay attention to *serendipity*—signs from the divine that show up in your life.

Serendipity is not just a fascinating movie idea; *it's physical evidence of a far greater reality.* Once we start cooperating with God and paying attention to the *signs* he shows us, we embark on an exciting adventure.

This compelling truth was proven to me in the most profound experience of my life, and it's been confirmed countless times over the last twenty-two years. The personal story I'm about to share with you has only been told to three or four close friends in my lifetime. The only reason I'm revealing it in this book is that I'm being spiritually led to do so. It's a dramatic illustration of this reality and the importance of signs.

❖ ❖ ❖

Sitting alone in my parents' den, my motionless body sank into Dad's recliner. I stared blankly at the ceiling as my sadness filled the room. Finally, I turned off the television to hear myself think. But the silence only intensified my isolation. How had I fallen so far? Life had lost all its joy; there were now only quiet, desperate moments.

Lost, confused, and disillusioned, I tried again to find where I'd gone wrong. I'd taken bold chances, been courageous, and followed my dreams. I wanted success badly enough, believed in myself, and had a positive attitude. Taking on a tough city and the most competitive business on the planet, I had gambled and lost. I felt betrayed, misled by this world; I'd taken its advice and failed. What was wrong with me? Was I not smart enough to figure it out?

Desperately, I searched myself for the person I used to be, but he was nowhere in sight. Shattered, broken, and bleeding internally, I hadn't seen my former self in a long time. A guy who was filled with feelings of failure, insecurity, and self-doubt had replaced him.

Having struggled with depression for a year, I was looking for a way to make the pain stop. I had read several self-help books, but nothing really worked to help me deal with the negative feelings that had grown to rule me. I was miserable; I wanted out of my body and mind.

I considered turning to drugs and alcohol to kill my pain, but instinctively, I knew this path would not bring me peace. Then I thought seriously about killing myself. Maybe this was the only way to make the pain go away. Would it really work? Would I just wake up on the other side, feeling better with a fresh start? It started to sound pretty good; the idea of some immediate relief even felt like hope.

PAY ATTENTION TO SIGNS

Next, I thought about my parents; they would be the ones to find me dead. And while I might be feeling better, they would certainly be unhappy for a long time, wondering if it was somehow their fault. I did not want to put them through that pain.

Suddenly, I caught myself. *What am I doing?* Right then, I knew something had to change. But after so many bad days, I had no clue where to turn. So what did I do? I prayed! I prayed and then prayed some more. I prayed for God to help me, to heal me, to make me strong again. I promised him that if he would lead me out of this dark place, then I would help someone else in the future.

After a while my heavy feelings lightened a bit; this relief gave me hope, so I stayed with it. I remembered as a kid feeling his loving presence, and I wanted to feel it again. I prayed for him to send me help and show me the path he wanted me to follow.

The great thing about desperation is that it causes us to actually start paying attention. A few days later, I was sitting in my office when a very interesting woman named Janet walked in. She was probably in her late fifties, dressed professionally, with a distinguished air about her. She emanated such an incredible sense of peace and harmony that I felt better just being in her presence. Fascinated by her charisma, I knew instantly that whatever she had, that's what I wanted.

Engaging her in conversation, I offered my help. She spoke in a smooth, calm, and patient manner. Her request was simple, so I handled it quickly. Then we began talking about other things. The conversation soon led to spirituality, as I was looking for a church that felt right to me. When I asked her advice, she smiled with a quiet knowing and mentioned that she taught spiritual-growth classes.

Intrigued by what she taught, given the powerful results she had obviously achieved, I asked her about the classes. She graciously told me a little about them and invited me to call her if I wanted to talk further. I did.

Walking into Janet's home for the first time, I was struck by the amazing peace that pervaded the room. I felt calm and comforted right away. I was impressed by the enormous home library that surrounded us—by far the largest I had ever seen. She also had a diverse collection of artifacts on display from her travels around the world.

As we talked, the depth of her knowledge, wisdom, and insight became increasingly evident. I had never encountered anyone like this before. We talked for a few hours, which seemed like minutes, then I told her my story and what I'd been going through. Her compassion was considerable; to this day, I'm deeply grateful that she took the time to help me.

At the end of our visit, I told her I wanted to attend her classes. She smiled and said OK, but she wanted me to meet someone first: Kathy, her teacher for the last twenty years, with whom she taught. Janet would make the arrangements and get back to me.

In a million years, I will never forget the events of the next meeting. We met at Kathy's home, where right away the conversation flowed easily. Kathy and Janet had been friends for many years and had traveled to forty-six countries together. Having experienced some amazing voyages, the depth of their knowledge about this world was remarkable. Spirituality, peace, and wisdom poured out of these women. I have never experienced anything like it before or since in my lifetime.

After a couple hours of intense conversation, the strangest experience of my life occurred. Sitting across from Kathy and staring directly into her eyes as she talked, I started to drift into

PAY ATTENTION TO SIGNS

this sort of dreamlike, surreal state of consciousness. Developing a bizarre type of tunnel vision, no matter how hard I tried, I could not look away. All I could see was kindness in her eyes and an angelic expression on her face.

Her lips were moving, but I couldn't make out what she was saying. Then my focus narrowed to just her eyes; all her other facial features became distorted and blurry. After staying in this state for a few minutes, I tried to shift myself in my seat but was completely unable to move. I just sat there, mesmerized by what was happening.

Finally, my focus widened and cleared a bit. I was able to pan over to Janet, who was sitting right next to Kathy and who had the *identical* angelic expression on her face. As my focus widened a bit more, I looked at both of their eyes, and I could see this current—this channel of energy—streaming out of them, pouring directly into me.

I'm not sure exactly how long this lasted, but it eventually subsided. Once again, I became completely alert and mentally present. The mood lightened, and we talked for a while longer on some less intense topics. But there was an unspoken awareness in the room that something extraordinary had taken place.

It had gotten late, so we said our good-byes, and Janet walked me out. I was wide awake and felt incredible. Every cell in my body was vibrating at an ultra-high frequency. Not sure if I should say anything, I just looked over at her with my eyes wide open and an exhilarated look on my face. She smiled and asked how I felt. She knew what had happened.

I told her I felt amazing. She said, "You feel like you've been let out of jail, don't you (referring to the disappearance of negative feelings that I'd been struggling with)?" I said, " Yeah, I do." She smiled again and said, "Well, good, you got a weekend pass," indicating that the effects of this powerful spiritual energy I'd just received would be temporary and that I would have to face old feelings again later. Remember, I'd been depressed for a year. But at that moment, I felt amazing.

I felt as if I'd been given a huge shot of spiritual morphine that completely washed away the intense emotional pain I'd been feeling. It was the most profound experience of my life, and I feel very blessed to have experienced it. Driving home in a state of euphoria, I tried to wrap my mind around what had just happened.

Then, completely out of the blue, I got this strange craving for mint chocolate chip ice cream—my absolute favorite as a kid. There had been a Baskin-Robbins near our house, and every year on my birthday, they'd sent me a gift card for a free scoop. I tried to think of an ice cream place on my way home. But when I looked at my watch, I realized it was almost midnight and nothing was open. I was almost at my apartment anyway, so I let it go.

When I got home, my roommate and his girlfriend were on the couch watching a movie, so I went into the kitchen to see what I could scrounge up. Like most twenty-three-year-old bachelors, we didn't have much in our fridge—just some lunch meat, a few condiments, and beer.

Then, I opened the freezer . . . and sitting there in all its glory was a pint of Baskin-Robbins ice cream. Wow, what a *coincidence*! I opened it—and which of the thirty-one flavors do you think I found? Yes, mint chocolate chip.

Who says God doesn't have a sense of humor?

Serendipity

Over the last twenty-two years, I've experienced hundreds of serendipitous moments like this one. Once we start cooperating with God, there are no "coincidences"—serendipity becomes a normal part of our life. These *signs* are his way of saying, "Stop and take notice; I am trying to show you something."

Serendipity is God's way of showing us he is actively working in our lives: opening doors, arranging experiences, and teaching us the lessons we need to grow. Sometimes serendipitous moments are funny incidents, just letting us know that he is there, helping us, and keeping us on the right path. Because our life is not a series of random events—it has purpose. If we are not paying attention, we severely limit our chances to be guided by him.

In retrospect, I can see that God was trying to reach me before this experience. But my interests were too absorbed by this material world. When our lives get busy, we develop tunnel vision and pass strange happenings off as "coincidences." For some of us, we must reach a point of desperation before we actually start paying attention.

Many people believe God created this world and directs the universe, but they fail to recognize his presence in their own lives. They accept this fact in theory but don't always make the mental connection between their inner thought-life and the events that occur in their life. Once you experience this reality for yourself and begin to attune yourself to it, you truly embark on a great journey. You see clearly and experience that this life is simply the reflection of a much greater reality. *Serendipity is the physical evidence of this truth.*

Our lives are just like a movie, with God as the director. The director works behind the scenes to produce the action that appears on the screen. He develops the script, arranges the scenes, and oversees the action, in an effort to realize the film's ultimate creative vision. He sees his stars' potential and tries to get them to deliver their best performance. He attempts to communicate with his talent and get them to share his creative vision for the movie. But he needs the cooperation of his star to make the film a success.

We are starring in the "scenes" of this human drama called life. To play our part effectively, we must pay attention to the director, look for our cues (signs), and stay focused during the scenes. If a star lacks focus and misses his or her cues, the scene does not work and must be repeated. It's identical to life, where we get the same challenges over and over—until we get them right.

God knows exactly which experiences we need to learn our lessons and move the story along. If the actor constantly ignores the director, production may have to be stopped until the actor changes his ways. In some cases, the director may have to cast a new actor to play the role that the original actor was selected to portray.

Now I'm not saying *everything* that happens in our world is a sign from God. Some occurrences are certainly the result of living in an evolving world of free-will beings. Choices made by selfish and self-centered people surely leave a wake of negativity that impacts the lives of others. Certain individuals have strayed so far from God that they've become evil. However, these persons who commit violent crimes, inflict abuse, and start wars cannot escape the universal law of cause and effect.

Furthermore, I don't think natural disasters such as hurricanes, tornadoes, and floods are God's will. Nor do I feel that medical disease or genetic imperfections in the human body are acts of God. Perhaps these are naturally occurring aspects of living in an imperfect, evolving world.

However, I do think God uses these happenings to effect positive change in our world. And there are many documented

PAY ATTENTION TO SIGNS

cases in which people received inner warnings about an impending event and avoided it.

What I'm saying is this: pay attention to incidents that strike you as unusual or coincidental, and seek to comprehend their meaning. When God is trying to reach us and teach us, he uses things that will get us to stop and take notice.

When we enter the path of spiritual growth and start cooperating with God, I believe he steps up his efforts to help us. Pay attention to things like these:

- You've been pondering a subject and then open a book to the exact page discussing it.
- You've been thinking about someone and he or she suddenly calls.
- You keep bumping into the same person over and over again.
- You unexpectedly cross paths with someone with whom you've had a previous connection.
- You go to bed with a question, and the next morning, the answer just pops into your head.
- You're studying, and something really strikes you as important or relevant to your life.

These are all things that make us go, *Hmmm . . . that's interesting*. When something like this happens, don't blow it off; ask for clarification about its meaning. Likewise, don't go nuts with it; always strive for balance in everything you do.

Just like when we take a road trip, *signs* are supposed to catch our attention and direct our path. They keep us traveling on roads already paved for us. Highway signs are not randomly placed; their location and timing are deliberate, particularly at important crossroads. It's the same for us, *especially when we're making significant choices.* If we miss our sign, we can get lost or end up traveling on rocky roads that make our journey arduous. And while every sign may not be a huge blinking neon light, even a subtle, well-placed sign keeps us on the right path.

God is constantly trying to reach us. Our lives can be like a movie, but we must play our part. If you have stayed with me this long, he is trying to reach you too. This is not the end—it's just the beginning. Enjoy your journey—it's a real trip.

8
DO THE GREATER GOOD FOR ALL CONCERNED

What if I told you this chapter contained the most powerful force in the universe? And that if you knew this *secret*, you could solve any of life's problems and make perfect decisions every time? Well, I've been using this principle for twenty-two years, and it has never failed. It works perfectly because it's a natural spiritual law.

This principle is the key to our spiritual progress and achieving the goals of this lifetime. You can apply this principle—the most important phrase you'll ever learn—to any situation, and the events will unfold exactly the way they are supposed to. If you will live in harmony with this one simple truth, you will generate true soul growth, gain wisdom more rapidly, and greatly improve your life.

While I realize these are bold statements, we are talking about the most powerful law in existence: the Greater Good for All Concerned. When we function in harmony with this natural spiritual law, we are perfectly aligned with the universal law of cause and effect. That's because God's will is *always* for the Greater Good for All Concerned.

In this chapter, we'll explore the role of this principle in moral decision-making and how to apply it, especially in challenging situations.

Moral Decision Making

The primary way we become more like God is through the act of moral decision making. God is an all-wise father who loves his kids equally. He is completely objective and *altruistic;* he does not indulge in favoritism. Given that the Greater Good is inherent in his divine nature, this principle is a naturally occurring spiritual law.

Our life is a series of decisions, whereby we have a choice to do what's good for us (selfish and self-centered) or do what's best for everyone involved (altruistic). Transcending, or rising above, our self-centered ways is the essence of spiritual growth. When we make decisions based on the Greater Good of All Concerned, we are functioning the way God functions. We are perfectly aligned with his divine will and this natural spiritual law. Thus, we become more like him, generating true soul growth and making real spiritual progress.

Moral decision making is also the method by which we gain the experience of human living. When we evaluate situations and act from the perspective of the Greater Good, we extract the true value of our experiences and acquire wisdom more swiftly. If we merely act out of self-interest, we don't learn anything of value. Wisdom is priceless in creating a better life.

The life we create is a reflection of our decisions. The Universal Law of Cause and Effect simply reacts to our moral choosing. This powerful universal reality is completely impartial and impersonal—like spiritual gravity. It's the true *intent* of our decision that determines our result. We surely reap what we sow; there is justice in the universe.

DO THE GREATER GOOD FOR ALL CONCERNED

I once worked for a company that went through some major operational changes that significantly impacted my quality of life. I was patient and remained loyal for several months as these changes took place, hoping things would get better. However, it became apparent that the situation was not improving, only getting worse.

Reaching a point where I'd lost all enthusiasm for the company, I knew the situation was not good for my family, the organization, or me. So I made the decision to leave rather than stay and simply go through the motions. And because my intent was truly for the greater good of everyone involved, I ended up getting a better job, with a better company, making more money.

When we make decisions based on narrow-minded self-interest, we reap the negative effects of our selfishness. We generate a wave of problems for those around us and ourselves. Then we must contend with these adverse results. If we don't learn from these experiences and if we keep repeating the same mistakes, we don't gain wisdom. We develop spiritual maturity by realizing that our decisions affect other people and by then changing our ways. Self-centeredness delays our growth.

The selfishness and greed of Bernie Madoff's legendary Ponzi scheme is a prime example of this fact. His decision to lie and betray many good people so he could lead a life of luxury created a tidal wave of financial destruction and landed him in prison.

When we act in harmony with God's will—this natural law, the Greater Good for All Concerned—we can *only* produce positive results. The forces of the universe are on our side every time. Our life flows smoothly, things just go our way, and we greatly improve our quality of life.

Living in harmony with the Greater Good also removes the inner conflict that results from the clash between our self-seeking human will and the altruistic urges of our higher spiritual nature. Aligning these two desires increases inner peace and promotes a happier life.

Growing up, I struggled with the concept of "doing the will of God." My resistance to that concept was partly due to my being rebellious, but mainly it was due to how the message was presented. Traditional churches I attended made it sound as if I had to give up my free will, which I cherished.

However, it's not that at all. Doing God's will is simply doing what's best for everyone involved, rather than what's just good for me—and I'm cool with that. I'm not saying that I never slip up, but I function this way most of the time. I simply try to get better each day.

If you come from a traditional background, the Greater Good is the ideal of the golden rule: do unto others as you would have them do unto to you. It simply means treating others like God wants them to be treated.

Objective Problem Solving

Using the ideal of the Greater Good makes it far easier to make decisions in challenging situations. Here are some steps to help you accomplish this.

First, try to clearly understand the situation you're trying to make a decision about. Think before you act; you need to be able to evaluate the situation objectively. See if you can track any problem to its source to get to the heart of the "real problem."

After identifying the problem, it's important to get your emotions and ego out of the way. We don't want fear, insecurity, or negativity to influence our judgment. This means avoiding

DO THE GREATER GOOD FOR ALL CONCERNED

reacting out of emotion, which inevitably creates more problems. Have you ever noticed how much easier it is to solve someone else's problem? And more fun too, don't you think? The answer's right there, staring them in the face, but they can't see it. We see it plainly because we're not emotionally involved in the situation; we are more objective.

Next, try to remove any personal feelings about the people involved in the situation so you aren't swayed by favoritism or personal bias. We want to treat everyone with fairness.

Now you're ready to make a decision that's best for everyone involved—based on the Greater Good for All Concerned.

At this point, we should remind ourselves to be tactful and compassionate toward others. We don't know what people are dealing with in their lives. They might be struggling with something that's driving the behavior creating the problem. I'm not saying it's an excuse, but it may be a factor. Remember, judge the situation, not the person.

You can see this situation play out in the world of sports, where you have an athlete with exceptional talent but who disrupts the harmony of the team. Coaches must evaluate the situation objectively and sometimes make the tough decision to cut a gifted player for the sake of the team.

Diplomacy and tolerance are valuable assets in improving our relationships and quality of life. Many times, how we deliver a message is just as important as the message itself in achieving a desirable result.

Dealing with stubborn people can test our patience, but the more skillful we become in this area, the better our lives will be. I'm not perfect here, but I've made a lot of progress. And I know from personal experience that self-mastery and self-control in this area take time and effort.

This process is extremely liberating because, once we

have gone through these steps, we can let go of the decision. The universe will handle it from there. We must learn to let go and let God. Occasionally, we think he needs our help, so we get back in there and mess with it. But trying to manipulate outcomes can interfere with our results, so just let him handle it.

Sometimes, it's beneficial just to leave a problem alone for a while. When a situation is complex or emotionally charged, we tend to overanalyze it—which just makes us more confused. Taking a break, especially doing something fun, can be very helpful. Oftentimes, we come back fresh, and the solution comes far more easily. It's like taking a mental vacation.

However, the most effective aid to solving life's challenges is entering a state of worship—taking feelings of gratitude to deeper levels of love, as we discussed in chapter 6. This practice restores our perspective, relaxes our mind, renews our energy, and strengthens our personality.

The key to successful living is having practical tools that help us solve day-to-day challenges. Objective problem solving and moral decision making are fundamental aspects of life. The Greater Good for All Concerned is the most powerful tool in existence. Apply this principle in your own life and you'll be astounded by the results.

9

HANDLE LIFE'S DETAILS

Employ thy time well if thou meanest to gain leisure.
—BENJAMIN FRANKLIN

Let's face it: we are comfort-driven, ease-seeking creatures. But if everything were done for us, we would never acquire the skills needed to accomplish our goals. There's a certain type of nobility we earn by taking responsibility for our lives and making our way in the world.

Handling the details of life stimulates practical growth in a way that leads us to develop noble character traits. Humble tasks propel us into the world to make decisions and solve problems. This training program helps us generate faith in our abilities, build self-respect, and become skillful at the business of daily living. When we learn how to be responsible, we become dependable—qualities that make us more like God.

Without the chance to handle the details, life may not work so well. For example, growing up, I met a really nice guy named Jake who, at the age of eighteen, had inherited millions from his grandparents. He was living in the lap of luxury: a house on the lake, a sporty boat with a private dock, and multiple cars.

Plus, his good fortune meant that he didn't have to work. I thought, *Wow, this guy has it made. I would love to trade places with him.*

Then a friend delivered some shocking news: Jake had recently tried to commit suicide. Stunned, I asked why a guy with such a great life would want to kill himself.

It seems that when the family estate had been divided up, it had caused a great deal of turmoil, with everyone fighting for their share. Jake had been the favorite, so he'd made out pretty well in terms of the inheritance, but the rift created between him and other members of the family had never healed. In fact, he tried not to talk to his family at all because they always wanted something from him.

Jake started to feel guilty because he hadn't earned his lifestyle. He hadn't yet become the person who had developed the ability to create it—a fact that jealous people reminded him of regularly. The guilt had finally become too much for him.

When everything is handed to you, objects lose their value. There's no sense of accomplishment. It would be like someone giving you an Olympic gold medal for which you hadn't trained, competed, or triumphed. What possible meaning could it have?

Handling life's details not only builds character and self-respect, it also improves our quality of life. When we take care of our details, things flow more smoothly. Details left undone create problems for others and ourselves—and then we have to shift into damage control to solve the problems, which further disrupts our peace. Many of life's problems result from someone not handling a detail.

Here's an example from my own life. My family owned a small cabin at Lake Whitney, one of the largest lakes in Texas. One day, when I was fourteen, my Dad told me that I could invite a friend and take our boat out by myself for the first time. As his words sank in, my whole world got still. My eyes widened with amazement, and testosterone raced through my body. In an instant, I had become a man; it felt like my Southern boy bar mitzvah.

It was an epic day—nothing but sunshine, blue skies, and smooth water. We skied my favorite spot, right before the Brazos River enters the largest part of the lake. We listened to music, soaked up the sun, and laughed all day. Finally, as the sun started to go down, we reluctantly decided to head back.

Just as we reached the lake's main entrance, conditions changed rapidly. The wind picked up, waves began to swell, and dark clouds rolled in. The boat started to sputter. Looking down at the gauges, I realized we were out of gas. I'd been so caught up in the moment that I'd forgotten to pay attention to that small detail.

It ended up being one of the biggest storms in the lake's history. Our boat was blown into a remote section of the river. We had no lights and no food—and a tree stump ripped our plug out. The Coast Guard rescued us at 3:00 a.m., on their final pass to look for us.

The next morning, returning to the scene, we arrived to find only two feet of the boat sticking out of the water. Yes, I had sunk the boat! But far worse than the loss of property was the opportunity I had lost to prove myself trustworthy to my father.

Trust is the foundation of all successful relationships. Being responsible deepens that trust. On a personal level, it allows us to strengthen our bond with loved ones, as they experience that we are reliable. It helps us to become a stable influence in our home, rather than create difficult situations.

Professionally, we earn the respect of customers and coworkers by honoring our commitments. Likewise, those individuals who have proven to be dependable get promoted. Clients gladly refer family and friends to people who are trustworthy. Reliability generates financial prosperity.

Running from our responsibilities only causes stress and anxiety. It disrupts our peace and makes life more problematic. Details left undone don't go away; they just stay in our minds until we handle them. There's no healthy way of dodging them, so we might as well simplify the process.

Simplify Your Life

> *Out of clutter, find simplicity.*
> *From discord, find harmony.*
> *In the middle of difficulty*
> *lies opportunity.*
> —ALBERT EINSTEIN

One of the best ways to ensure that we're able to take care of our responsibilities is to get organized—a profound way to simplify our lives. *Personal organization makes life easier and more fun; lack of organization creates chaos.* If we look for ways to accomplish tasks most efficiently, it becomes more of a game. Every check we make as we mark things off our to-do list feels good, because we don't have to think about it anymore. Then we can get back to the things we enjoy most.

Some of the most powerful inventions in history have been created to help us manage our lives: smartphones, laptops, e-mail, and the Internet. And while I use these innovations to complete many tasks, I prefer to manage them with my day planner. Putting pen to paper just works best for me. The system is simple, reliable, and effective; goals, monthly tasks, and daily duties are all in one place. My organizer makes me feel in control of the day.

But it doesn't matter what approach you use—life's way too busy *not* to write things down or enter them into your system. Trying to manage all your tasks in your mind creates mental clutter, increasing your stress and complicating your life. Personal organization helps us stay balanced. It provides structure that supports creativity and enhances our ability to improvise. It liberates us by creating time for what matters most.

Your goals should be an expression of what's most important to you. Each morning, simply review your goals and monthly task list, as you create a game plan for the day. Assign a level of priority to each task. Having a goal and a clear strategy makes many details take on new meaning, and identifying the weight of each detail increases effectiveness and promotes equilibrium.

You're now prepared, focused, and ready for the day. If an urgent matter comes up, no problem, handle it and get back on track.

Don't become obsessively organized or too rigid with your schedule. If an opportunity presents itself to have lunch with a friend, and it's not going to create any major challenges, go have some fun. If you don't get everything done that day, simply slide the unfinished tasks to the next day and handle them—no big deal. Just stay focused on the higher-priority items so they don't cause problems down the line.

We all wish that we had no responsibility at times—that's normal. And it's certainly important to balance our striving with recreation. But if our lives were *too easy*, we would be lazy and unproductive, and we wouldn't develop strong character. It's for our own good that we face responsibilities—it makes us better people. If everyone were idle on a regular basis, the world would be filled with a bunch of flakes and slackers—and we already have enough.

It's about finding balance and having the right tools in place. Successful living is about having practical methods for dealing with the challenges of everyday life.

> *Most people struggle with life balance simply because they haven't paid the price to decide what is really important to them.*
> —STEPHEN COVEY

APPENDIX A

HELPING OTHERS— ACTS OF KINDNESS

Sharing valuable information is one of the most powerful ways we can help those around us. If you feel this book's content is important, then I encourage you to become a partner in this effort; please share it with your friends, family, neighbors, and coworkers. Look around your sphere of influence. Right now, people you know are dealing with situations that can be greatly improved by applying this book's principles.

The Internet and social media empower you more than ever to have a positive impact on those you care about. It takes only a moment to share a quote, book, or website that has resonated with you. Not only is this *act of kindness* a potent stimulus for your growth, but you just may change someone's life.

I also encourage you to be aware of customers, clients, and fellow coffee lovers at Starbucks who might benefit from this material. It's a very nice gesture to buy someone a cup of coffee, but the gift of vital information has a far greater potential to impact that person's life. In our busy lives, there are many instances in which we cannot sit and talk with someone for hours. But it only takes seconds to direct someone to a good book that offers helpful advice.

Over the years, I've kept extra copies of certain books on hand and either loaned them out or given them away. This practice of *paying it forward* has sparked some very interesting conversations and has assisted many people. I hope this book is like that for you. One of my primary reasons for writing it was to provide a valuable tool for individuals who desire to help others.

Likewise, this book is not meant to be a one-time read. It's intended to be a faithful companion, a compact guide of principles to help us stay on track. Our life's journey is filled with potential distractions and detours; there's great value in having a compass to help us maintain a proper direction.

Thank you for reading my book and embarking on this journey. *I really hope you enjoyed it!* Please visit my website and blog at www.bobbyfite.com.

APPENDIX B

THE GUIDE TO SUCCESSFUL LIVING

To live in harmony, always keep the following summary of this book's principles in mind:

- Apply Your Faith, Desire, and Persistence to the Right Principles
- Develop A Balanced Money Perspective
- Manage Your Estate of Mind
- Be the Real You
- See the Big Picture
- Awaken Your Spiritual Energies
- Pay Attention to Signs
- Do the Greater Good for All Concerned
- Handle Life's Details
- Share Valuable Insight with Those Placed in Your Path (Helping Others)

APPENDIX C

THE TOOLBOX: TOOLS, TECHNIQUES, AND STRATEGIES

In chapter 4, I stated, *The key to managing our state of self is replacing a negative FEELING with a positive FEELING!* Replacing a negative feeling takes more than a *single* thought *impulse* or even a few thought impulses. A positive feeling is created by a *series* of positive thought *impulses* that grow into a positive *feeling*.

We get "into" a positive feeling by allowing the positive energy generated by our thoughts to saturate our entire body, then staying immersed in this positive energy until the positive feeling is solidified. Then, the negative feeling fades away, and we feel better.

Here are some techniques you can use to help you replace a negative FEELING with a positive FEELING; or, stated another way, to help you get back "into" a positive state of self.

Setting Goals and Dreams

*If you want to be happy, set a goal
that commands your thoughts,
liberates your energy, and inspires your hopes.*
—ANDREW CARNEGIE

Goal setting is one of the most powerful tools I've used over the years. We all greatly benefit from something we can plug into our mind that gets us pumped, excited, and feeling good! The ongoing advantage of using this tool is perhaps even more valuable than achieving the goal itself.

Here are a few key elements of this process:

First, select a goal that's big enough or compelling enough to excite you. It can be anything you would *love* to do: build your dream home, ski the Swiss Alps, take a dream European vacation, or have your own business. Just find something that excites you; the key is generating positive energy.

Next, it's important to write your goal down in a way that's attractive to you. It should be well defined, with a clear strategy for achievement. Drawing an inspiring picture of the goal is also extremely helpful. I don't tend to be a particularly visual person, so I really benefit from visual aids to help me form a mental picture. This clarity and visual appeal is very stimulating and confidence building.

When you look at your goal, imagine what it would feel like if this dream came true. Assume the FEELING of having already attained this goal. *This is the most important part of the process.* Becoming immersed in this positive feeling is the key to getting back to a positive state of self.

In getting started, don't get too caught up in whether you

APPENDIX C

think you can do it or not. You can gain benefit from the technique simply by creating the feeling of what it would be like to have attained your goal. In fact, if you don't have any goals set, then you can create a dream scenario that helps you get "into" a positive feeling. For example, what would you do if you had $10 million dollars? What kind of life would you be leading? I've had some success with this technique, but imagining my actual goals work better for me.

I'm certainly not the first person to talk about the power of goal setting. So why don't more people set goals? I think there are a few reasons.

First, they simply haven't taken the time to do it. It takes some time and effort to sit down and decide what's important to you. But it's fun! And Franklin Covey has some very good goal-setting tools to simplify this process.

Second, they don't want to feel disappointed or criticized if it doesn't happen. OK, I get it. I've been there, so let me share some thoughts and ideas to help you get past this.

Adopt a nothing-ventured, nothing-gained attitude. Don't attach your personal happiness or self-worth to the accomplishment of the goal (see chapter 2). I'm not saying don't be committed to your goal—persistence is key. I'm just saying relax, have some fun with it, and see what's possible. You never know what's possible until you try. What do you have to lose? Nothing. What do you have to gain? Everything . . . including the benefits of using this tool, and this is very important. This lightness of being will help you generate positive energy and make it easier to succeed.

Don't tell everybody what you're going to do—just do it. If you share your goals with anyone, only do it with people who support and encourage you. Keeping a low profile with your plans takes the pressure off. Besides, most people are so busy with their own lives that they really don't care all that much. Always under-promise and over-deliver.

It's funny how people look at things differently. Many people don't set goals because they worry about them not coming true. I'm exactly the opposite; the idea of having no goals in life is far more troubling to me. Having no direction is much more concerning than knowing where I'm headed. In fact, a few years back, I accomplished a few substantial goals I'd set for myself and didn't get specific about any new ones for nine or ten months. I just didn't know what I wanted to do next. I felt off-balance, and I didn't like it.

In my opinion, our ultimate goal is pursuing a life of purpose; using the attributes of our true self in a way that improves the lives of others.

Gratitude and Worship

Entering a state of genuine worship, which is simply taking feelings of gratitude to deeper levels of love, is a powerful tool for creating self-transformation. This process strengthens us, renews our positive energy, and helps us return to a positive state of self. I could never have transformed my life or myself without this strength-giving practice.

Love is the most powerful energy in the universe. By allowing feelings of love to saturate our body and by staying immersed in this positive energy, our negative energies must dissipate, dissolve, or fade away. The key is remaining in this highly desirable state long enough for this transfer of power to happen.

Repeating this experience allows us to reach deeper levels of peace; it strengthens our sense of self, modifies negative energies, and elevates our internal vibrational level or "peace threshold" (the normal level of peace we feel on a day-to-day basis). In short, worship makes us feel better and improves our ability to remain in a positive state of self.

Early in my growth, I created a list of things I was thankful for and used it to start my daily meditation time. This routine eventually developed into a spontaneous event, but in the beginning, the list was a helpful tool. I still refer to it occasionally to make sure I don't forget anything. This list—along with high-quality spiritual books, quotes, or excerpts—can be an effective aid to worship. Likewise, I try to worship in nature whenever possible. There's more on the subject of worship in chapter 6.

Positive Re-Minders

> *Strong, positive affirmations are a powerful*
> *means of self-transformation . . .*
> *Every thought you think and every word*
> *you say is an affirmation.*
> —JACK CANFIELD

Affirmations—or positive "re-minders," as I prefer to call them—are strength-giving statements that help you generate positive energy and return to a positive state of self. They are well-crafted assertions or *a series of thoughts* that are particularly empowering to you. They're like Red Bull for your mind, a quick burst of energy to help you generate power.

Affirmations can be goal, life, or self related. They are stated in the present tense, assuming they are a current reality, and often begin with words like "I am . . .". They are simple, relatively brief, and to the point. Here are a few examples:

- I am a positive, happy person who feels relaxed, charming, and charismatic.

- I live in the loving presence of God and attune myself to his leadings.

- All things are possible with God. The universe wants me to succeed.

As you repeat, affirm, or *re-mind* these thoughts, you want to *imagine feeling that way.* You want to re-experience or *assume* the feeling they create. This technique is basically what actors do when they get *into* character.

In the book *Unlimited Power* by Anthony Robbins, he asks, "Have you ever had the experience of being on a roll, the feeling that you could do no wrong?" (p. 46) You may want to create some re-minders that help you attune to this state. How do you feel when you are at your best?

Activity tends to help generate energy. Therefore, you may find it helpful to add some motion to this process; try moving around the house or office as you use this technique. Likewise, there's more information on affirmations in *Jack Canfield's Key to Living the Law of Attraction.*

Please keep in mind that these self-reminders are only effective to the degree that they help you generate a positive feeling inside, a feeling that can be solidified until the negative one fades away—*this is the key.* If you are unable to generate a positive feeling at times, then I recommend transitioning to one of the first two techniques. In my opinion, the second tool offers the deepest level of transformation. After all, love is the most powerful energy in existence.

You can also use or add a collection of inspiring quotes to this technique to help you generate positive energy.

APPENDIX C

Taking Action

In some instances, you might need to combine action with these techniques.

The area of health and fitness is like this for me. If I've been working long hours, eating on the run, and missing workouts, then at some point, I must simply take action. I can only put it off for so long, and then I cross a threshold and only feel better once I've handled it. Afterwards, I'll use one of the tools if needed.

A few years ago, I went to the doctor and had an MRI done after five months of daily back pain. The photos showed that I had three herniated discs in my lower back, and it looked as if I might need surgery. This was a huge wake-up call, as I'd never experienced a health issue that sidelined me from activities I enjoy. If you're healthy, be thankful and take care of yourself.

In my opinion, there are two types of challenges we deal with in life: those we can change and those we can't. For those we can't change, well, I think the wisest strategy is to simply try to let go of them, stay focused on the positive aspects of our life, and play the cards we are dealt to the best of our ability. (And have some fun doing it!) I mean really, what's the alternative—making ourselves miserable over things we can do nothing about?

For those areas we can change, especially those that are important to us, I feel we always benefit from taking action.

❖ ❖ ❖

If you've felt off for a while, you may need to repeat this process until you get back on track. Be patient with yourself as you work with these tools and elevate your internal state of feeling.

I'm a practical person; I go with what works. Sometimes, I like to work with one technique for a while and then transition to another in order to keep things fresh. I suggest you find what works best for you.

Please note I am not a PhD; I speak from a perspective of life experience and my own personal changes. If you have deeper issues that keep resurfacing and causing you difficulty, then you may also want to consult a professional counselor. Seeking out help is not a sign of weakness; it's a sign of intelligence. Life's too short to be in a regular state of dis-ease, so do what you need to do to get past it.

ACKNOWLEDGMENTS

I would like to thank all the people who, over the years, have loved me, supported me, and made me laugh.

First and foremost, I'd like to thank God for the countless events he has orchestrated in my life. He's been a faithful companion who has always seen the very best in me and had my best interest at heart. Thank you for trusting me with this important work; without you, none of this would have been possible.

Next, I'd like to thank my loving wife, Kristen, for believing in me and supporting me during this purpose-driven project. Thank you for realizing that this endeavor selected me and was not born out of personal ambition.

I also want to thank Jeff Johnson, my great friend and true brother for 22 years. He has always been ready for any adventure and has come into it with an all-in attitude. Never underestimate the value of a true friend.

I would like to thank my parents for their love and willingness to take on the challenge of raising a rambunctious kid. And special thanks to my father, who passed away while I was writing this book, for letting me try stuff and always having my back.

In the literary world, I want to thank Jennifer Read Hawthorne, my editor, for her skill and expertise in helping me actualize this book; Carol Kline, my writing teacher, for her kindness, compassion, and insight into the writing process; and Dan Poynter, for his pioneering spirit and practical books that help new authors get their message out.

And last, I'd like to thank all the musicians, actors, writers, comedians, filmmakers, spiritual teachers, leaders, and philosophers who have had the courage to follow their dreams and share their gifts with this world. Your inspiration has fueled many great endeavors.